the
PLATINUM
in the
POISON

Stories and Resources from a
Year of Chemotherapy

HANNAH KATE FORD

First Edition copyright © 2025 by Hannah Kate Warner
Second Edition copyright © 2025 by Hannah Kate Ford
Cover design and artwork by Hannah Kate Ford
Cover copyright © Hannah Kate Ford
All rights reserved.

Harmonic Press
Harmonic Resources, LLC
Chapel Hill, NC

Published by Harmonic Press, an imprint of Harmonic Resources, LLC. The Harmonic Press name and logo are trademarks of Harmonic Resources, LLC.

Publication Data
Name: Ford, Hannah Kate, author.
Title: The platinum in the poison: stories and resources from a year of chemotherapy/ Hannah Kate Ford.
Description: Second edition.|North Carolina: Harmonic Press, 2025.
Identifiers: ISBN 979-8-9924431-7-2 (hardcover) | ISBN 979-8-9924431-4-1(paperback) | ISBN979-8-9924431-5-8 (ebook) | ISBN 979-8-9924431-6-5 (audiobook)

For Elsie and Bea

Contents

Introduction

The world is filled with poison.

Some days we feel the pain so intensely. There is war, and hatred, and violence. Grief pulls us under, anger pierces our communities, blame permeates our language. There are toxins spilling into our water systems, fires and floods raging through our neighborhoods, depression and anxiety incapacitating us.

In 2020, the world shut down and we moved into a most-peculiar quarantine existence to avoid the poison of the COVID virus. We all had additional poisons to deal with on top of the pandemic. My extra poison was chemotherapy.

In February of that year, I was diagnosed with stage IV Gestational Trophoblastic Neoplasia — a rare cancer that was a direct result of my second pregnancy. It is an aggressive but usually curable form with a low recurrence rate. I began my cancer journey in hopes of seeing the finish line within four months or so, but with my progressed form of the disease it took much longer than I expected. In the end, my cancer treatment lasted just under a year, with a total of 21 rounds (42 infusions) of multi-drug chemotherapy plus two of immunotherapy.

I had been struggling with other poisons, too: anxiety, grief, and exhaustion. I began the year already worn down by life. Cancer treatment forced me to address these poisons alongside the physical drip of chemo.

I know what it is like to be tired and achy from the medicine, to feel scared and powerless and lonely amid a harsh and toxic physical experience—but I do not know what it is like to be given a scarier prognosis. This is one of the lenses through which I write.

Cancer required me to move away from regular routines and focus inward. There was no way around this. It was exhausting and disorienting, and also a tremendous opportunity to dig into the deeper layers of my existence. The body, mind, and spirit are profoundly connected, yet modern Western medicine tends to break them up and treat the body in isolation. Beyond the physical experience there is a depth of reality—of the self, the other, the natural world, and a Source that is beyond it all. This is what I refer to when I use the word *spiritual*: the experience we have when we journey past the surface. Chemotherapy was an intensely spiritual voyage into spaces I had never reached before.

I spent the year thoroughly digging— into my past that was affecting my present, into resources and ideas that would support integrative cancer treatment, into my own existence in ways that I could not have foreseen. This was the only way through cancer during quarantine.

On the other side of it, I see everything differently. I am changed, and life has become more expansive, curious and fun. I have learned to dance with the wind of Mystery and Unknowing. We are all trying to figure out what it means to be human—to find meaning and purpose in this confusing earthly reality. It is often the hardships that offer the perspective we need to move forward, brightly engaged with life.

If you are going through or about to go through chemotherapy— you may be fearful, unsure of what to expect, and concerned that you will never feel like yourself again. It is true that it is a holistically intense experience. There will be layers upon layers of challenges mixed with joys. I am here for encouragement and cheerleading—to tell you it is possible to get through the poison and recover to your best, brightest self. My hope is that my transformation might offer some sense of potential for you, too.

Each cancer is a unique disease, and the drugs that go along with them are also unique. I cannot guarantee that your results will be the same as mine, and I am certainly not here to offer a cure for your cancer. Here I will share the tools and resources I have found that I believe can support your experience no matter the specifics of your disease. Addressing the spiritual and the material together is the key.

One of the most potent ways I have healed—from chemotherapy, from anxiety, from loss—is through stories. Reading books and hearing spoken words have helped me to feel not-so-alone in these dark places. I have learned to harness the power of sound, of color, of movement, and of fun in my years of recovery. Through creative expression and meaningful engagement in life I have found a deeper soul healing.

In the pages that follow, you will find stories from my year of treatment intertwined with all my best resources for surviving chemotherapy. Many of these tools came from the "wellness living" I was working with prior to my diagnosis, and I am certainly grateful for the resources that I have from that space. But I needed to come to a balanced point of realizing wellness was not quite enough. I needed resources that would permeate into my deeper being. As a result, I share some resources that are practical and material and others that are more clearly in the realm of the spirit. This book truthfully represents my eclectic journey with chemotherapy.

I needed all these tools at various points in my treatment to come through the year intact. There are many resources listed at the end of each chapter, but they are not meant to be used all at once—that would be very stressful. Just take what you need and leave the rest. The spiritual resources engage the elements of the natural world through meditations, sound healing practices, storytelling prompts, visual art and movement exercises. You will also find practical advice and tools—specific recommendations that include supplements, nutrition, and healing protocols. I hope there is a little something here that will be of service to you on your journey through the poison.

The stories that follow are mine, yet they belong to others too. The words were gifted to me by a great many people, by experience and by time. I hope my own storytelling might inspire yours—the telling and hearing of our stories together is an act of healing in itself. Though my memory is not always accurate, I do my best to share truthfully the details as I remember them. Most of all I seek to offer words that might temper the loneliness. Courage arrives in community: we all have our stories of poison.

I believe that there is possibility in this world beyond what is right in front of us, beyond our ideologies, structures, and solid forms. Buried in our challenges, we find our greatest meaning and resources for the path ahead.

When I looked deep into the poison, I found something that sparkles: the world is filled with Potential.

May you find it, too.

Prologue: Poison

Grandmother Mary died at forty. I was told since I was young that I am like her— not quite five foot one, indelicate hands and a hot temper, also kind and generous, warm and funny, full of music.

Mary played the organ in rural eastern Kentucky while my grandfather preached in a Southern Baptist church. She left behind four children—my father was the oldest, nineteen at the time of her death—and an ancestral legacy of anxiety that pervades my family. The 1970s Western medical system did not understand her health challenges, and they all suffered for it.

Grandmother Mary was largely a mystery to me growing up. There were very few photos of her around; no one spoke much of her. I gathered bits as the years went on: she struggled with her health, both physically and emotionally. She was given drugs that were largely toxic and seemed to make things worse. Poisoned, on some level.

Her death was by choking.

I came into the world by way of an emergency c-section, the umbilical cord wrapped around my neck three times, choking.

"Motherhood killed her," my dad told me once. He spoke these words to me as I held my first baby daughter a decade ago, in the throes of postpartum anxiety. My father has a great many talents, but timing is probably not one of them.

Would motherhood kill me, too?

❦

It was the middle of the night, and I was nineteen years old. At Centre College—in the center of Kentucky in the small town of Danville—I hemorrhaged out my throat a week following a tonsillectomy that had not healed properly.

I arrived at the emergency room, bleeding at an alarming rate. I sat powerless in a tiny room full of fluorescent lights and busy people, my chest and arms caked in blood, wondering what was going to happen to me. My skin grew gray and wrinkled from the loss of blood. They jabbed me with needles over and over trying to find a proper vein in that windowless cell.

For too long, there was not a doctor there who could help. This little hospital did not have an ear, nose, and throat specialist on call.

That was when I first felt it: *panic*. It began at my toes and quickly seeped up through me until it reached the top of my head. Breath was hard to reach, and I felt myself sink into a state of disorientation and crushing fear.

Eventually, they found a local retired ENT doctor who could help. He entered the ER and looked at me.

"Am I going to die?" I asked him slowly.

"No..." he answered, with a quick aversion of eye contact.

They wheeled me off into surgery, and the last thing I remember is an anesthesiologist at my side, asking if I was in a sorority.

❦

I didn't die. But I had medical trauma to deal with, and I didn't realize it. Intense panic attacks became a regular experience for me in the years that followed. I dealt with sometimes incapacitating fears of death, powerlessness, and needles. My anxiety hit full form after college graduation as I embarked on a life journey in which I could not see two feet ahead of me. Alone with my degree in mathematics, I felt constantly as if I were teetering on the edge of death.

Disoriented and dissociated, I moved back to the suburbs of Louisville where I had grown up, bouncing from medical specialist to medical specialist trying to fix myself. Finally I turned to what I call *wellness living* with significant success. I was 25 years old when I found an amazing acupuncturist, changed my diet drastically, read the entire 784 pages of *Healing with Whole Foods: Asian Traditions and Modern Nutrition*, and began my journey into feeling better. I love books, so I read every book I could find on holistic healing, nutrition, energy work, yoga, meditation, and herbalism. I read about panic attacks and anxiety and depression. I decided I would need to avoid Western medicine as much as I could if I wanted to be healthy.

I arrived in Durham, North Carolina in 2010 to attend Duke Divinity School, feeling well but still lacking direction and purpose. Divinity school was a mixed experience for me, but panic was generally low during those years. I was still gripped by my fear of death, though the expression of it was no longer full-blown physical panic. On my school breaks I found myself reading books on cancer and its treatment and prevention. It seemed that those who were dying young were dying of cancer. I desperately needed to avoid this early death, so I rabbit-holed myself into amateur cancer research. I spent time as a hospital chaplain intern on the cancer floor at Duke University Hospital; I taught yoga classes with cancer patients at the local cancer support center. I graduated from divinity school three years later, still in a state of professional disclarity.

c◯◯◯ɔ

Marriage and parenthood both arrived in 2014. The birth of my daughter, Elsie, presented new joys and challenges. With mothering came another expression of anxiety. It was a smashingly beautiful experience for me, full of love and panic.

As I learned how to parent, far away from my Kentucky home and from my family, the challenges continued. In 2016 my cousin, Robert, who was more like my brother, died in a car accident and I was left with a gaping hole in my heart that I didn't know what to do with. He was one of the only people on the planet who crossed the family-friend barrier and always made me feel okay to be myself. But with the busyness of new motherhood, I lacked a space for expressing my grief. It began to fester.

⌒∞⌒

My second daughter, Beatrice was born in 2017—months after our family moved from Durham out to a farm twenty miles west in Mebane. I thought the farm would bring me a sense of calm spaciousness. Instead, I was overcome with pounding isolation.

I struggled with motherhood even more following this second birth. I felt a connection with my daughters that was so true and eternal. Simultaneously, I experienced deep shame and guilt about myself as a mother. I felt like a mother failure. I was sick; something was not right in my body. Sometimes my insomnia hit so hard that other people had to step in and care for the children. Mothering was my job; for five years it was my only job. It was what mothers were supposed to do, I thought—take care of the children all the time and in all the ways. It was supposed to be the most joyful task I would ever have. I had failed at that, for some days the joy of motherhood was nil. The exhaustion, overwhelm, and drain of motherhood were what I felt. *If this is the experience, something is surely wrong with me,* I thought.

I took to calling it *smotherhood*: that feeling of non-breath, of choking. It was a somatic experience in my lungs and in my throat that I felt when I couldn't catch a break or a moment. I lost my focus and my sleep. The emotional task of being in charge of two people was more than I was able to handle. All of the responsibilities of modern parenting—even the simplest of tasks—sometimes felt impossible. Feed little humans, clothe them, bathe them, read to them, make sure they are actively engaged with nature. Make sure they are doing art. Don't put them in front of screens. Only give them healthy food. Speak to them. Sing to them. Give them the right colors to look at. The right music. Make sure they have play dates and learn to socialize. Pay attention to their habits and keep an eye on whether there might be something amiss. Early intervention will be best if something is not right. Make sure all this is done with love in my heart because if they don't feel that I love them all the time, then they will not develop a proper attachment. *If they don't develop a proper attachment, they will become anxious, like me.* I did not want them to be anxious like me.

Whether I was with my children or not, these responsibilities weighed on me deeply. When we were together, I was high-strung, and when someone offered me a break, I still felt responsible, now with the added guilt of not being with them. I lacked a feeling of purpose, and felt my identity lost in the jumble of motherhood. I felt powerless and confined and so guilty for feeling this way. Respite seemed impossible.

In the fall of 2019, I began teaching math part-time at the Waldorf school in Chapel Hill where my daughter, Elsie, was in kindergarten. I thought it would balance my life as a parent. In many ways it did—I found a new brightness in entering a classroom at a beautiful place. But by winter, the continued weight of feeling like a mother-failure had taken over once again.

As 2020 began I was still so tired. My body had felt off for a long time. It had been over two years of more-intense-than-usual imbalance, but I thought I was living the wellness life. I ate organic food, had a farm below my feet. I meditated, exercised, took my herbs and supplements. I had my organic mattress and my electro-magnetic field checker. My toothpaste had charcoal in it; my water was fluoride-free. Most importantly, I avoided Western medicine as much as humanly possible. I was careful. And I was worried. *Wellness living* had begun to stress me out more than it was helping me.

My insomnia returned. I felt dense and lethargic, and the anxiety was palpable. It didn't seem like I was a person capable of both parenting and having any semblance of a life outside of it. My body felt slow, as if filled with thick tar. My lungs and my throat were tense and restricted. Physical and spiritual poisons had settled into my being—fear, grief, shame, purposelessness and isolation.

Smotherhood.

It felt like motherhood was killing me, too.

Light

It was the middle of the night, and I was 35 years old. I couldn't sleep again. Insomnia was a regular experience for me, so the darkness had become a comfortable sort of enemy. The little farmhouse with wooden floors creaked quietly as I moved about while the rest of my family slept soundly in another room. It was still outside. Chilly, probably.

I stood in the bathroom and stared out the window at the 22 acres of land we lived on. Full of beauty, and also pain, heartache, and difficulty. I felt the isolation in my entire being. The seclusion of the farm setting had worn me down.

It was February 24, 2020. My daughters, Elsie and Beatrice, had both come down with a virus, and I caught it, too. I had been home sick from my job teaching math at the Waldorf School in Chapel Hill for a week now. The girls had healed up, but my sickness hung on. I had a nasty cough, and I fumbled through the cabinets looking for something that might help. I fell into a coughing fit, and it turned so gnarly that there was blood. I had coughed up a bit of blood a week earlier, and it had sent me into a spin of concern. Family members had told me not to worry; I was a historic hypochondriac, after all.

But this time it was not just a little bit of blood. The blood kept coming, and I could not stop coughing. Quarter-sized globs spewed out my mouth, filling tissues until I finally realized I needed to get to the emergency room. My spouse at the time, Matt, drove me there,

21

while his mother—who was thankfully in town for a visit—came to be with the girls.

I called my own mother from the car in a state of slow panic on the way to the hospital.

"Pray for me," I told her. "I'm coughing blood. And I'm really scared."

My parents were in Kentucky; they had a home in both states and oscillated between them. She said she would start driving as soon as she could get herself ready. My mother, Lisa, is always quick to pray and quick to show up, even if it means a nine-hour car ride in the middle of the night.

The drive to Duke University Hospital was a tense and scary experience. I knew there were prayers holding me in some fashion, but my fear was too thick to feel them for long. Instead, I nauseously swam in my anxiety, an experience that was not new to me. Neither was the blood spewing out of my mouth in the middle of the night, and for awhile I drifted off to that time that I had hemorrhaged from my throat. Images of nurses frantically digging needles into my arms filled my imagination.

I knew that I couldn't steep in the fear, in past experiences. I knew it in my mind, but the rest of me was having trouble. I was numb, shutting down, focusing in on the reality of the blood expelling out my body again. I stared out the window at the blurry lights of the interstate. I was quietly scared out of my mind.

I was admitted to the ER quickly and put through basic blood tests. There was a lot of waiting and not much information. Next, there would be a chest x-ray. I sat in the patient room, nervous and coughing, wondering what could possibly be happening to me.

Eventually, a nurse arrived with a wheelchair to take me off for the x-ray, but before I could sit down in it a young doctor whooshed in and pulled us to the side. He needed to tell us something before I could go.

He was a little jittery—not unusual for someone who has to work the night shift in the ER.

"Um...I am not sure if this is good news for you...um. But...um...you're pregnant." He looked up at me, hope in his eyes that this would be good news.

"No I'm not," I said bluntly.

"Yes, you are!" Now he was getting happy about it. He looked down at his clipboard, like he needed to check again. "Yep...you must be four months along or so." He told me I likely had a bronchial infection combined with a little being coming to life in my body.

"Ummm...." I thought about this one. "No. Nope. Nope...not pregnant." I would definitely know if I were four months pregnant. This was the weirdest fight I had ever had.

"Well, hmmmm. Well." He looked at me, like he was trying to figure out whether I was being serious. I was. "Let's get you an ultrasound, then."

I held this puzzling news for a while. I felt confident that I was not pregnant, but as I waited for the ultrasound technician to arrive, I let myself go there. *Okay, if I'm pregnant—then what? Whew, Bea is only two years old and Elsie is five. We hadn't planned to have any more. It would be tiring, but we would be okay. Maybe it would be good, even. Yes, it would be good.* In my imagination, I decided that she would be another girl and we would name her Louisa. *Elsie, Beatrice, and Louisa*—three sisters. They would certainly have fun together.

The ultrasound technician went to work.

Sure enough, no baby.

Someone wheeled me back to my room in the ER. Then there were more tests. Another round of blood was drawn, I got that x-ray, I had a CT scan. I waited.

Young Squirrelly Doctor came back.

"You were right," he tells me. "You are not pregnant."

Not pregnant—no, actually, I had cancer. Cancer that has spread. He didn't have any other details. He was sorry to have to tell me this. He looked at me awkwardly. I can't remember if he stayed or if he left.

Cancer?

I was stunned.

"Elsie and Bea, Elsie and Bea, Elsie and Bea..." was all I could say.

I experienced a whirl of confusion and disorientation as I held this incomplete information. I tried to consider what this meant. If I had metastasized disease throughout my body then surely I only had months to live—my children would grow up without a mother. I sank into a state of shock and nausea.

Elsie and Bea, Elsie and Bea, Elsie and Bea.

It wasn't long before they wheeled me away again. This time it was for a brain MRI—they were concerned that my cancer had spread there, too. From what I could gather, this would all be even more troubling if it had hit my brain. I had been in an MRI machine only once before, a decade prior when I had been experiencing constant disequilibrium. I remembered that clicking tunnel as someone moved me to a different room in the interior of the hospital. I tried to mentally prepare myself for an uncomfortable, claustrophobic situation.

I reached a windowless room and saw the machine. My stomach churned as they helped me climb onto the table. I would need contrast, too—tingly color they would put into my veins through an IV so they could see all the brain details more clearly. Color in my veins was not part of my wellness living regimen. I lay there, looking upward toward an uninteresting ceiling. Someone asked me if I was okay. *Sure, I guess? I have cancer, and that is all I know. I am not sure that* okay *is a possibility, but...yeah? I guess I am okay.*

The noisy clicking began. I felt the movement into the tunnel. I was attached to tubes and needles and electronic gadgets. I had already been so thoroughly poked and prodded. I felt non-human with all these bits on me, just one patient of many in a similar predicament. There was no way out of this tunnel, so all I could do was take a deep breath, close my eyes, and try my best to relax. I entered the cold, cream-colored, sterile vortex. All the way into the tunnel I went as the clicking grew louder. The voice through the speaker in the tunnel told me that the scan was starting and to please be still. I felt cold and alone. Confused and scared. Powerless.

But I allowed myself to sink into the table, to search for calm in my body while in this tunnel. Words floated into my consciousness, not from the speaker but from that place of depth from which wisdom flows intermittently:

I am bathing in the light of God.

The words came with a tune, a song I knew from somewhere in my past called *We Are Marching in the Light of God.* But I was bathing, not marching, and that one line repeated over and over as I lay in that tunnel. *I am bathing in the light of God. I am bathing in the light of God.* I felt myself bask in a swirl of brightness, of peaceful feelings. I imagined the light seeping into my body, filling me with love and warmth. Part of the experience came from an internal place, but another part was external. I lay there so calm and silent, with a touch of a smile spreading on my face. I was alone as could be in a clicking tunnel machine with artificial color spiking my insides, knowing I had cancer, and yet in that moment, I was unafraid. Past the anxiety and the loneliness. Somewhere brighter, to another layer of existence for a time.

When I made it back to the patient room, I felt different. The calm brightness was residual. I wasn't in the swirling space of light anymore, but there were sparks left over in my being. Something had begun to break in me, a touch of the deep fear of death had dissipated. Given the circumstances, I felt somehow steady, and maybe even, *okay*. I had bathed in light in an MRI machine, and for a while all was well.

What is this light I bathed in? It came from within and without, not visible to another human but a clear experience for me. Light is an odd sort of substance. Its natural sources are sun and fire, lightning and twinkling fireflies. Light is so necessary to our sight that sometimes we don't even notice it. It bounces and reflects, it creates shadow, it brightens that which is held in darkness. It moves and dances. It forms our vision. It is light that fills the infinite sky by day and sprinkles it with stars by night.

Throughout history, people have worked with and pondered the mystery of light. They have learned to bend it, to reproduce it in some fashion, and have theorized about what it is made of and from where it comes. Ancient mystics saw light as God itself—until the 1600s, the accepted idea was that light was indeed an expression of God, a holy manifestation of the Divine. Then modern science brought new ideas about light, the way it is subject to the laws of physics, the way it can be broken into colors or gathered together.[1]

Now we stare at fake light all day on our computer screens, our iPads and our phones. Our offices and classrooms buzz with fluorescent bulbs that help us see but somehow aren't quite right. The screens that addict us seem to be essential tools for modern society. I'm using one to write this book, and I know how difficult it is to find the balance. Light is complicated.

The outdoor, natural world seeps with light—sometimes in wide open splashes and other times in smaller streams and speckles. The Divine Light can trickle into us or bathe us in brightness. In any form, light illuminates our path.

⌒◯⌒

They wheeled me back to another little room, and we waited for some information under fluorescent bulbs. We were told that it would arrive soon. I was already uncomfortable—coughing blood, so exhausted—but the waiting made the discomfort more substantial.

Finally, a woman in a white coat arrived. Dr. Allison Puechl was tall and poised, young, with long blonde hair. I knew she held my fate on her clipboard as she carefully sat down to explain this situation to those of us in the room. A couple of friends, perhaps my mother, and my spouse were there. The details were fuzzy as I continued in a state of shock. Dr. Puechl laid out the information with hopeful clarity.

It was true that I was not pregnant. The cancer I had was stage IV Gestational Trophoblastic Neoplasia, a form of chorio-carcinoma. It is a rare thing, this cancer. Bodies are strange and fascinating, and the biology of it always brought me into puzzled curiosity. A tiny piece of placenta, the sac of nutrients that had been feeding Beatrice more than two years earlier, had been left in my body. Usually, this cancer is caught soon after giving birth and sometimes during pregnancy. The time that had elapsed between the birth and the diagnosis was long and unusual, one of many reasons why I was considered *ultra high-risk*.

At some point, this little bit of placenta had started growing and moving and wreaking havoc in my body. What began as nutrition for my child had transformed into poison for me. It became tumors filled with the pregnancy hormone *human chorionic gonadotropin* (hCG), which was why my initial diagnosis was pregnancy.

The cancer had spread to my lungs, where there were many small tumors scattered about and a mango-sized one in the middle of my chest. I had other tumors on my spleen, liver, and spine. I was fortunate that at Duke University Hospital—the closest medical facility to where I lived—we had one of the only oncologists in the country who specializes in this cancer, Dr. Brittany Davidson. I would be in good hands, Dr. Puechl told me, and I would meet her tomorrow.

I was also told that I needed chemotherapy immediately. The globs that were in my lungs were the most worrisome. Those who died of this cancer usually died in the first weeks after diagnosis of breathing complications since this cancer tended to set up shop in the lungs. There was no time for wellness living or second opinions. This cancer was very aggressive, and it had already spread all over my body. It was growing at an exponential rate and we needed to act fast. The poison of chemotherapy was the only option.

The chemotherapy would begin with two induction infusions of cisplatin and etoposide. Then I would move to a weekly cocktail they call EMA-CO. The first week I would receive the EMA:

etoposide, methotrexate, actinomycin D. I would always need to spend the night at the hospital to receive these drugs. A week later, I would receive the second half, the CO: cyclophosphamide, vincristine. For these, I could come into the Duke Cancer Center clinic for an outpatient infusion. One round of chemotherapy equals two weekly treatments. I was told that I would likely need six to eight rounds, but it was all up to my hCG levels—the pregnancy hormone that would be my cancer marker.

I did the math. I love math, but not this kind. Six to eight rounds of chemotherapy meant I should be done with treatment by June. Summer would come and I would be free. I just had to make it through these few months.

The cancer part was scary. But I admit I was even more afraid of the chemotherapy. *What would it be like to knowingly fill my body with toxins? To be bald and frail? Nauseous and sick? Unable to care for my children?* I had read enough books on the subject to know that people didn't just die from cancer; they also died from complications of the treatment. This was really going to mess with my wellness living. Poison for healing did not make sense.

Dr. Puechl brought details, and with them more light. The light of hope was a high probability that this cancer would be cured. I knew how lucky I was.

∾⦚∾

I sat blankly with all of this information. It was so much to hold, even with an excellent prognosis. I felt it in my whole body. I coughed more blood as I let it sink in.

And then the girls arrived in the ER room: Elsie and Bea. Two-year-old Beatrice had crazy, curly blonde hair at that time. Naturally silly, dynamic, and tiny—she is flowing and flexible, with a watery nature. She has big blue-green eyes that shift their color depending on the light or on what she is wearing. Elsie was five years old, with light copper-colored hair and freckles. Her slate blue eyes are almond-shaped and she has a seriousness about her. She is intense, analytical, and sometimes explosive—bright as can be. She is my fiery one. My children are as different as day and night—sun and moon.

I was so relieved to see them; their smiling faces brought peace to my whole self. I was also weak and achy knowing that they were going to have to go through this, too. They were going to watch me be sick, and they were too little to understand it. I was drenched in mother guilt. But their presence brought a tranquil shimmer to the thick, chaotic energy of the ER.

⌒∞⌒

The sun illuminates our entire existence from the center of the solar system. Light is central to life on this planet—it feeds the vegetation on the earth and it feeds us, too. Without it, we would not exist. Natural light transmutes our inundation with scattered, artificial light. It is the antidote to the blue and fluorescent hues that modern life steeps us in.

Light meditations have been used for millennia in various spiritual traditions. Visualizations of light would profoundly hold me for the next year. To turn my attention to light was so simple, and so powerful. The physical, emotional, and spiritual effects of this turning were palpable.

My year with cancer began with light. I would learn to lean into the light during my treatment —slowly toward a mysterious, divine Light I can never fully understand, and toward the light of outdoor sunshine and brightness all around. The observation of light and the experience of its movement in the world became a great healer. Light is an invaluable resource when journeying through the toxic confusion of chemotherapy. Developing a conscious relationship with light can ease tension in the body and position the spirit toward bright curiosity.

Light

Get Some Sun

Spend time in the sunlight to counter the time indoors, especially if you spend a lot of time in the fluorescent lighting at the hospital. Try for an hour a day outdoors, but as much sunlight as you can get will be beneficial. It is particularly important to spend at least twenty minutes outdoors before 10 a.m. to keep your circadian rhythm functioning well. A balanced rhythm will help your body more readily heal from the treatment.

Bring a Lamp

If you must be in the hospital for an inpatient stay, I highly suggest bringing a small, non-fluorescent desk lamp for lighting. Softer, warmer light will keep your nervous system calm during treatment. Anything you can do to lower stress during this time is useful.

Decrease Blue Light Exposure

Find balance by minimizing blue light exposure to increase your body's natural rhythmic and healing capabilities. Listening to audio meditations or music, journaling, drawing, or talking to a caregiver are all excellent alternatives if you find yourself overdoing the blue light of screens during treatment.

Observe Light and Create

The simple act of observation can be a powerful experience when the internal world is wrought. Draw your attention to the light in the natural world around you—the way it moves, creates forms, and speaks its own language. Take a photograph or paint an image of the way light expresses itself in nature. Let the light that you observe permeate your consciousness.

Bathing in Light Meditation

Find a comfortable position sitting or lying down. If you are in a moment of challenge or chaos (getting a scan or poked with a needle, perhaps), tap into your inner self and find the place in your body that feels the most comfortable and safe. Focus on this space.

Close your eyes and take three deep breaths in and out of your nose, slowing your breath with each inhale.

Visualize a wave of light coming from outside of you. It may approach from above or below, or you may feel yourself fully immersed at once. Invite the light to enter in, whatever form and method it takes.

Allow that light to expand so that it holds your entire body. Feel yourself wrapped in the warmth of this golden, bright light. Let it swirl so that you experience yourself in the middle of a vortex of light. This light is full of love and hope.

Hold yourself in this light bath for as long as you would like. Breathe slowly and steadily.

61 Points of Light Meditation

Lying down in a comfortable place, palms facing up with your legs about hip-width apart, take a few deep breaths to settle in. When you are ready, imagine a drop of warm light at each of these 61 points on the body:

Point between the eyebrows, hollow of the throat, right shoulder joint, right elbow joint, middle of the right wrist, tip of the right thumb, tip of the index finger, tip of the middle finger, tip of the fourth finger, tip of the small finger, right wrist joint, right elbow joint, right shoulder joint.

Hollow of the throat, left shoulder joint, left elbow joint, middle of the left wrist, tip of the left thumb, tip of the left index finger, tip of the middle finger, tip of the fourth finger, tip of the small finger, left wrist joint, left elbow joint, left shoulder joint, hollow of the throat.

Heart center, right side of chest, heart center, left side of chest, heart center.

Solar plexus (space below the breastbone)

Navel center, right hip joint, right knee joint, right ankle joint, right big toe, tip of the second toe, tip of the third toe, tip of the fourth toe, tip of the small toe, right ankle joint, right knee joint, right hip joint.

Navel center, left hip joint, left knee joint, left ankle joint, left big toe, tip of the second toe, tip of the third toe, tip of the fourth toe, tip of the small toe, left ankle joint, left knee joint, left hip joint.

Navel center, solar plexus, heart center, hollow of the throat, point between the eyebrows.

Chapter Resources

Continue breathing deeply as you experience this warm light throughout your entire body. The light holds you closer to the earth, in peace and brightness.

Enjoy the sensation of warmth, deep rest in your body, and brightness in spirit for as long as you would like, ideally at least 10 minutes.

Breathing Light Meditation

Sitting or lying down, settle into a comfortable position. Take three deep breaths in and out of your nose.

Bring your attention to the bottoms of your feet. Feel light tingling and brightening those two points.

On your next inhale, feel the light move all the way up both legs, into your hips, through your pelvis, through your core, to your chest, up your throat, and all the way through your face to the very top point on your head.

As you exhale out your nose, the light moves down in two streams through the sides of your head to your shoulders, all the way down both arms to your elbows, your wrists, and leaves your body through your fingertips.

Inhale again through the bottoms of your feet and repeat.

Continue this cycling of light and breath for at least 10 minutes.

Chapter Resources

Centering Prayer

This is a simple, old form of contemplative prayer that can bring connection to the Divine Light and insight into the Self. Find a quiet place and give yourself at least 20 minutes to sit with your eyes closed.

Allow a sacred word to arrive by way of your intuition. It is just one word that you will focus on during this simple prayer meditation time (you can use *light* if nothing else comes to you).

Invite awareness of and deeper relationship with a sacred Light.

Come back to your sacred word if you find yourself swimming in thought.

That's it![2]

Circles

It was January: a month before my diagnosis.
I was driving my children home from school. I was exhausted. We were traveling on the interstate in the minivan when a little spot appeared in my vision.

Then several spots.

The spots expanded until they became black rings—circles in my vision field. I was terrified. I could barely see enough to drive—my whole body flew into a panic. It had been awhile since my last panic attack, so I panicked, also, about the panic itself.

Fortunately, we were almost to the exit ramp and our house was less than a mile away. I was able to send a *help me* text, get the girls out of the van, and tell them that mom was not feeling well and needed to lie down—*please play by yourselves for a little while.* I found my way into my bedroom, lay down and closed my eyes. The circles were still there.

Circles, nothing but circles, for an hour.

When they finally subsided, I was left wondering what on earth could be wrong with me. *A brain tumor?*

It turned out seeing circles is called an ocular migraine, and that was the first of several that I experienced in the weeks leading up to my cancer diagnosis.

I was pushed in a wheelchair from the emergency room to the main wing of Duke University Hospital —the ninth floor. This was a familiar place for me: I had spent the summer of 2012 there as a hospital chaplain intern. I had specifically asked to be assigned to the cancer floor because I thought facing it might help me break through my fear of early, tragic death and of cancer. Apparently the universe was unsatisfied with this gesture. For those months, I wandered these same halls, checking in on people whether they wanted me or not. It was an experience that helped me to see clearly that I did not, in fact, want to be a hospital chaplain.

Now I inhabited one of these hospital rooms as a patient. How quickly my identity had shifted in these past twelve hours. *Cancer patient. I am a cancer patient.* I was so disoriented by this truth. Everything and everyone around me whirled and buzzed; those first few days were abrupt and confusing.

Some time elapsed; there were many more tests. They wheeled me out of the room a couple of times—zooming me around the hospital in a daze and eventually landing me back on the ninth floor.

Stillness settled in as evening filled the room and we waited for the chemotherapy drugs to arrive. During the day there had been visitors—family and friends and my two little girls. But as the darkness fell, it was just my family of origin: my mother, father, and sister, Claire. It wasn't often that it was just the four of us for anything these days.

The induction drugs were etoposide and cisplatin. They were harsh but a lower dose to ease me in. It would take many hours to receive the medications by way of an IV in my arm, so I was told to get comfortable in my hospital bed. *Comfortable?* There was nothing comfortable about this situation.

I whirled and swirled out into that space of imagination and of questions: *What was this going to be like?* It felt like I was living my worst nightmare, like I was stuck in some alternate-reality horror film. *Why was this happening? What is going on with me? What is going on with the world? Am I really about to get poison dripped into my arm? How did I get here?* I was tense, and yet I still felt the peculiar teeny bit of light, a touch of brightness intermingled with all the questions out in my dream space.

The drugs arrived. The nurse kindly asked how I was doing and hung them up on the IV stand. The nurses were all special and wonderful; I could always feel the genuine care on the ninth floor. I wish I could remember their names, but I would meet so many over the next year that they have been lost in my memory.

I looked at the bag. I suppose I received one drug, one bag, at a time? (I did this so many times...why don't I remember?) I stared at the bag—considered what was inside of it, imagined it streaming into my body—and I felt pale.

It was almost time for the drip to start. I tried to breathe calmly and slowly. I let out a big sigh. *I think I can do this. And if I can, then... there is healing on the other side of this experience.* I knew this deep in myself. I was in desperate need of healing. And somehow, this was going to allow it. I felt this sparkle of hope as I sat uncomfortably in that hospital bed.

My family formed a circle, and time and space shifted. For a while, the circle transported me to another place.

My family is from Kentucky. Many of my ancestors lived in the rural eastern part of the state. I was born in the middle of it and then moved to the suburbs of Louisville to do most of my growing up. I migrated to North Carolina in 2010 for school, thinking it would be temporary. I love North Carolina, and I also miss my Kentucky home. My roots in the land of my grandparents' farm in Lewis County run deep—this place is an extension of myself, as if its dust particles are permanently stuck to the bottoms of my feet. Much of my childhood was spent walking the fields and the hills, exploring the spaces and marveling at the interesting history of the land.

There had been others at that farm with us. My mother had two siblings, and there were always cousins running around. Some lived just up the road, others lived out of state but would visit as often as they could. My mother had a sister whose children were Robert and Meredith. We would become like siblings over the years through our woven, sometimes tragic, paths. Robert was just a year and a half older than me, so we played together a lot as children. We fought, as do all people who are close enough to love one another. We laughed and played games, joked around with our trickster grandfather, Papaw, and made cookies with our grandmother, A.A. We explored the farm together. In the evenings, we played Rook with our mothers.

It was a whole different world there, slow and peaceful and full of love. Country and sweet. But with an edge—the roughness of hard farm work I could feel in my Papaw. I loved Papaw, and I knew he loved me too even though he'd never say it. I knew he loved me because he called me Kate. It's not my middle name, so I'd ask him why he called me that.

"Well, I don't really know," he'd say in that kind, soft country way he had about him. "You just seem like a Kate to me."

And that always seemed true to me, too. Kate was playful and a little bit country; she walked on the gravel barefoot, climbed trees and rode cows. There was something particularly shiny about me when I was Kate. I always felt like I could be myself around Papaw, and his peaceful energy was subtly guiding.

There were several barns at the farm, but one main barn we thought of as Papaw's. Sometimes I stood around in it watching him work. I loved the smell of the tobacco and dirt floors. I loved the way the barn was dark but light still trickled in through the cracks in the panels. I understood why Papaw loved farming: it is hard work, and it is good work. To be with the land and the animals, to work in that barn—what a different life he had than mine. And how I could have stayed in that barn and been happy for days.

I loved A.A.—Alice was her name—in a different way. She felt tall to me, though she couldn't have been particularly tall. She was direct, a bit firm even, and strong—my maternal line is filled with strong women. She had long thin legs, and I always wondered why I did not receive those when I was dealt my DNA cards. Beautiful green eyes. She would cook and sew, keep everything tidy, create beautiful quilts and cross-stitched pieces. But you sure did not want to mess with her. Do not let the kitchen door slam, and do not make a peep during Papaw's nap time. Do not complain about your food, or anything for that matter. There was a tree out on the side of the yard that I loved to climb. I would climb it every day when I was there, spending hours reading in it or developing an intricate imaginary world. A.A. called it *Hannah's tree* and I liked that because it meant I got to decide who climbed in it.

Back in the hospital room, it was 2020 and that country, childhood world didn't exist anymore—at least not in the same form. My grandparents had died. Robert and Meredith's mother—my Aunt Marilyn—had died, too, after a long experience with frontotemporal dementia. My mother had inherited the farm, but it was hard to take care of from a distance. She had to sell it, and it felt like the farm had died. Robert had died not long after that. The people I loved, the land I loved, the barn and my tree just weren't there anymore. It felt like an abyss of grief in my spirit.

There we were, the four of us—The Warner Family. And these losses that I have written of were not the only ones we had faced. As all families do, we had experienced a web of challenges, some individually and some together. We held grief and anxiety; we had struggled within ourselves and with one another. We were four strong personalities, and sometimes that was hard. We also loved each other a lot, and that was palpable in the room on this particular day.

We sat in a circle, and we prayed and offered gratitude.

And the poison started to drip. *Drip, drip, drip.*

When the chemotherapy began, a weakness filled my body. I could feel it percolate, creating an eerie hollow feeling. Like liquid filled with tiny shards of glass. It felt harsh, and I soon experienced a full body ache. I felt myself become weak. It is difficult to adequately describe to anyone who has not been through it—certainly not akin to any of my previous experiences, but closest to a really, really bad hangover.

We all sat for a while together, but there wasn't much to see. Eventually, Claire and Dad left, and it was just my mother and me sitting in the little room. She was in the recliner with a blanket, and I could tell how tired she was. She was likely in desperate need of some sleep. This would be the first of many, many nights that my mother and I would sleep in the same room together in the coming year. She moved into our little farmhouse and slept next to me in a recliner, or on the couch in the living room, for the duration of my treatment and some months after.

It was quiet, but the chemo continued to drip. *Drip, drip, drip.* Every once in a while, something beeped. *Beep, beep, beep.*

"How are you feeling?" She asked me, kind of groggy-like.

But it wasn't *how* I was feeling that was so strong in that moment. It was *who* I was feeling.

"Hmmm...." I thought about it. Felt it all wash over me. "Well, I'm feeling the ancestors. I feel A.A. and Papaw and Robert. And I feel like this is going to be okay."

"Yes...the veil is very thin right now. I feel them, too." She told me.

My mother, Lisa, is a thoughtful, perceptive human. Spiritually attuned to others and to that which lies beyond. In her eyes—which are sparkling green with a striking limbal ring—you can tell that she sees far past the material surface.

I had thought about my ancestors before. I certainly missed them. In hindsight, I had felt them, but I didn't name it as that. But now I *really* felt them—their spiritual presence in that room. My maternal side was especially strong on this particular night.

⌒∞⌒

Growth rings within the trunk of a tree came to mind. Each circle represents time —the oldest circle on the inside and the newer ones toward the periphery. The inner circles are smaller, aged. They are the hardest to access from the outside, but they lie within that vital, most stable part of the tree. Our families and our ancestors must be this deepest inner circle. Within this circle we are often faced with challenges that help us grow; the inner circle is not always the easiest place to be.

On this first night of chemotherapy, my circle transported me. Time and space expanded, and I felt how love exists eternally. Our spirits morph in ways we don't understand, and death is just...a transformation of sorts. I could feel the possibility of infinite existence on that night. This world—the journeys we are on—is part of a grand soul adventure. Those people I loved were with me. I felt this in a strong and transcendent way. The circle held me and I knew I was part of it—no matter whether I lived or died.

⌒∞⌒

Papaw had given me old coins over the years and so I had a well-stocked collection. The one I loved the most was the 1922 silver dollar. 1922 was the year that he and A.A. were born, and the image on the coin was a liberty head. As my treatment continued, I was drawn to this coin more and would hold that circle in my hand during meditation or chemotherapy. I felt truly connected to my Papaw through this coin. Occasionally, I would misplace it, and it would return exactly when I needed it. In the coming year I would feel the cosmic comedy of my trickster Papaw seeping through time. I learned later that this coin is fittingly named the *Peace Dollar*.

❧

The circle is infinite, proportional, strong, and connected. The mathematician in me is deeply fascinated by circles. They are a historic, ancient symbol of continuity and connection. The circle is a transporter—when we connect with people in this way it is like we can shift time and space.

❧

During my year of treatment, my family of origin held me and loved me and took care of my children. My circle of ancestors was a vital resource, too. My medical team —the invaluable doctors and nurses at Duke University Hospital—provided me with brilliant care. I held my circular coin. I noticed the circles present in nature. I created my own circle of complementary practitioners to support me in different realms of healing. There were people outside of my immediate family who regularly checked in on me—most often my friends Leah and Megan, my Uncle Chuck and my Aunt Terry. I am so grateful for all of these circles.

Accessing circles was necessary for my healing. Every human needs connection in some form, and the intensity of chemotherapy necessitates that you learn what works for you. Not everyone experiences the self and the world in the same way, so finding the unique circles that are supportive for you is part of the task. There are many possible circles and ways to connect that might support you through cancer treatment.

Circles

Connective Object

Use an object that is meaningful to you as a comfort piece during chemotherapy or any moment of treatment. If you do not already have one, speak aloud your need for connection and security, and look for a sign. If you speak this need without specificity, an object may show itself. Perhaps it will even be circular.

Visual Art Circles

There is something calming about sitting with the visual of a circle. Paint, doodle, and meditate on the shape itself. It will hold you.

Practical Medical Circle

I highly recommend pulling in an integrative or naturopathic doctor as well as practitioners for complementary care. Find people you resonate with who can weave together a circle of support.

Spiritual Circle Meditation

Find a comfortable seat or lie down. Take several deep breaths and release any tension.

Feel yourself grow warm—radiating the light.

In this place of glowing, deep consciousness, you are able to encounter the circle of support that you need for your journey. You call in your circle.

Chapter Resources

Allow yourself to be in a place that you know. You know it because you have been there before, in the material or the spiritual world. It is a place of rejuvenation and nourishment. It always holds exactly the resources that you need to flourish.

Sink into this place and feel the details of where you are. There may be colors or forms, objects around you, or parts of the natural world. Look around with your internal vision and feel the love that this place holds for you.

This is your place of full support, and you feel it in your entire being.

You are now joined in this place by others. They are your circle. They might be family and friends you recognize, ancestors and angels, guides and mentors. They are the ones with whom you travel. Always there for you in this space of resourcing and transformation.

Experience each of them with all your senses, know how deeply you are loved and supported in this circle. Experience their encouragement, their brightness, laughter, and wisdom. You are joyful and held in this place, with these beings.

Stay here in this circle as you continue to relax in deep awareness.

When you are ready, say thank you and goodbye to the circle, receiving what you need for your journey into your heart. Slowly move back into awareness of the present moment and space.

Dust

The first chemotherapy infusion continued
into the middle of the night, the wee hours of the morning on Ash
Wednesday. In the Episcopal Church where I grew up, I would
have gone to a service to mark the beginning of Lent. It is the
commemoration of Jesus fasting for 40 days in the wilderness
before his gruesome execution. A priest would have put ashes on
my forehead and said:

> *Remember that you are dust,*
> *and to dust you shall return.*

Dust, indeed—just a speck I am. Dust is light enough: made
of earth and air, the light flitters through it, making it appear
simultaneously breathy and heavy. It was humbling and soothing
for me to consider myself a speck among many other specks on
this particular day. *Remember that you are dust.* Mortal, fallible,
imperfect. Also, a part of something much larger.

~⊗~

It is a peculiar thing to try and sleep while on a chemo drip. I
would learn to do this in the year to come, but at first it seemed

impossible. Sleep was already difficult enough for me. *Drip, drip, drip.* I could feel it making its way into my body. The hospital room was never silent. *Beep, beep, beep.* Beeping is one of my least favorite noises of all time. Sleep? Surely not.

When morning arrived, the drip was over. It was still just my mother and me in the tiny hospital cell. I felt that hangover-like sluggishness, some nausea, and this bizarre sort of hollowness in my body. But I perked up as I sipped on a glass of spirulina, the blue-green algae I had been drinking as a health tonic for a decade. I started feeling kind of smug. *Chemo? Eh, I was fine. What was the fuss about?* I wanted to go out for a walk, so I took a stroll around the hospital and landed back in my room feeling more refreshed.

My mind was foggy, though. This entire first week in the hospital is still jumbled in my memory. It was a whirl of medical tests, infusions, and doctors and nurses. I can't tell you for sure when I met Dr. Brittany Davidson, but it was likely this morning. Dr. Davidson would be my main oncologist, and I heard her enter the room: *Click, click, click.* She usually wore heels. She was small in stature, with beautiful dark hair. A strikingly pretty human with a clear sense of fashion. She must be about my age. She is firm but very kind and has a depth of emotional competence paired with intellectual brilliance. She is funny. She is also pregnant with her second daughter, she tells me. Later in the year she will go on maternity leave, but she hopes that I will be finished with treatment before then. Her visits are always quick—she *click, click, clicks* in and out of the room—but they ease my tension. It is true what Dr. Puechl told me in the ER: I am in good hands with Dr. Davidson. I hear another doctor in gynecological oncology refer to her as "Brit," so I do too, in my head. After our visits I often find myself flying out into that dream space, imagining the life of Brit when she leaves the hospital room. There must be fancy dinner parties and fun of all sorts to counter her serious life as an oncologist. Maybe a fur coat and a fancy hairdo. Dangling diamond earrings.

The highest of heels and a long cigarette that is just for show. I find her to be a fascinating human—she is a mother *and* a professional and she seems to be doing it all with style. She does not appear to be having panic attacks.

After my visit with Dr. Davidson and others, my blood work came back, and my hemoglobin was low. Someone told me matter-of-factly that they would be giving me a bag of blood to get that number up and make me feel better. I thought I was feeling pretty good. *A bag of blood? A blood transfusion? Someone else's gooey insides?* This would be the first of many bags of blood that I would receive over my course of treatment.

Blood.

When we hear the word, our minds often go to violence and death: *bloodshed, bloody battles, bad blood, blood and guts.* It is the stuff that spurts out of us when we are wounded, and it hurts when that happens, so it also represents pain. Many people can't stand the sight of blood. We would like for blood to stay in our bodies, please. It isn't usually something we swap with one another. In fact, that is highly discouraged.

In Traditional Chinese Medicine (TCM), the blood is the nourishment of the body, circulating the vital energy *qi* (pronounced *chee*), which I knew from all the acupuncture I had received over the years and from my amateur studies of TCM. *Deficient blood* was often a challenge in my body, according to this understanding of health.

Blood.

I would get this substance dripped from an IV bag, like all the medications I had received so far. But this one used to be part of another human whom I did not know. A nurse brought in the bag and hung it where the chemotherapy had been. It looked healthy, a dark red color. *Whose blood was it?* I would never know. Someone with the same type of blood that I have: O positive. That is all the information I would get. This person could have been local or from farther away, old or young, kindhearted or mean, robust or dry. I sifted through all the possibilities. Would it be just the physical blood I would receive? Not according to Chinese Medicine—I might also receive the invisible life energy—the *qi*.

I did not want someone else's blood. The idea made me feel kind of...*prickly*.

But I realized I did feel kind of weak, even if I was high on spirulina. I was also used to feeling this way. I was historically slightly anemic, a little tired even if mostly quite active. I was certainly more drained in specific situations—being indoors too much, constant chattering or mind-work, lacking music or movement are all stagnating for me. (Writing this book is making me a bit lethargic, too).

The IV started dripping again. *Drip, drip, drip.* Into my arm, a little bit at a time. This transfusion would take an hour or so. I just sat there, in the hospital bed. *Beep, beep, beep.* All I could do was receive it—receive the help, and be grateful that I am not dead.

When it was finished, I did feel better. I had more energy, rather suddenly, but the calm kind. I felt refreshed and...flavorful? Yes, *flavorful*. Like my insides were unflavored before, and now I had flavor.

I had received my first round of chemotherapy, a bag of someone's blood, steroids, codeine for my cough, and an anti-psychotic drug that they use for nausea called olanzapine. As someone staunchly opposed to prescription medication at that time, this reality was dizzying. I had to come to terms with my physical needs for all of these interventions, and that was a daunting task in itself.

Acceptance became a necessity. I wanted to fight the medical system, say no to chemo and run off to a cancer clinic in Tijuana. I truly believe there are alternative routes in some cancer cases. I can also say that on this side of the experience, my case was not one of those. I needed the Western medical system for my aggressive, chemo-sensitive cancer. I needed the poisons of all kinds, and I needed the blood of others to keep me going.

Remember that you are dust.

I had to accept help, and that was my first challenge. I had been programmed toward independence. I believed it was of the highest value. To need help implies a weakness of character, of spirit even. I want to do things on my own, to carve my own path, to take care of myself. Dependence is frowned upon in some of the circles in which I have roamed, and creates situations in which others are owed. Usually, if someone offered me a kindness, I always felt deep within me that there was a string attached. Accepting help was uncomfortable. I did not like being sick and having others swoop in to take care of me. I wanted out of this mess as quickly as possible.

I would learn, slowly, to come into acceptance of the present, to open myself to the help of others in many forms. Whether it was medicine, blood, childcare from my sister, money from my father or coconut oil foot rub/prayers from my mother, I was forced to receive help. This was a lesson I needed to learn, and that I am still learning.

Dust. Mortal, fallible, imperfect—mortals must accept help.

All I could do was just relax into the experience and receive. There was not another option at this moment.

Mortals must accept help, yet hold strong in themselves. This is the balance, and it is challenging for me still. Dust is a balance of earth and air—so I had to receive the blessings of sky while also standing my ground. Perhaps I am not the only one who struggles to be strong and independent, and also willing to receive help. It is delicate.

Remember that you are dust.

Dust

Accept Non-Acceptance

If you struggle with this one like I do, the first step is to accept your own lack of acceptance. From this place, what is needed to become more accepting of help? This is a thought experiment.

Stream of Consciousness Writing

This is a simple yet powerful technique for somatic awareness and accessing inner guidance and intuition:

At the top of a page (in a journal or on a blank sheet of paper), write this question:

What do I need to accept?

Look at the question, then close your eyes and breathe deeply for 2-5 minutes.

Allow your thoughts to flow freely, coming to a place of quiet stillness. Focus on your breath, breathing in and out of your nose. After you have settled for several minutes, pick up a writing utensil and answer the question by writing *without stopping* for 15 minutes. Set a timer if you need to, but do not stop writing. If you find yourself veering off topic, draw your focus to the question at the top of the page. Just write and allow the flow without thinking too much about it.

At the end of 15 minutes, read what you have written.

Chapter Resources

Spend Time with Dust

Whether it is with the trees, the creatures, the plants, the mushrooms, the flowers, the moss, or all of it at once—spending time with the earth and air and all of their life forms helps us feel connected to the whole. Sit with the beauty that is there and let the strength permeate your being.

Breathe deeply and slowly as you experience yourself as an imperfect mortal.

Now inhale and gather a sense of empowerment and strength from the earth around you—from all the bits of dust. Exhale and let your breath join the sky.

Repeat and repeat.

Try a Mantra of Acceptance

Speak aloud what you hope for yourself in this realm. Perhaps *it is okay to accept help*, or *we are all in this together.* Or, *remember that you are dust.*

Repeat this mantra to yourself as often as you can.

Energy

My first stay in the hospital lasted seven days.
I was released from the medical world for a moment, and I seemed to be doing okay with the chemotherapy. I felt well enough to move around and go places as I began adjusting to this new reality. I only had one day before I would receive another infusion of the poisons—this time in the outpatient clinic at Duke Cancer Center.

I wanted to take care of myself really well. I had high *wellness living* standards that I was convinced I needed to meet. I knew I could support myself with nutritious food, exercise, meditation, and sessions with my holistic care providers. I thought that surely, with these tools, I could get through this in record-breaking time and be able to move on with my life. I desperately wanted to move on with my life, so I dove head-first into all of the resources I had, trying to implement them all with exuberance.

The truth was that I believed in healing. I believed in fast healing, despite anything our modern medical system might say about that. I believed that wellness living could fix anything. I had read a hundred books on these topics and had been working hard to heal myself of all sorts of issues for most of the past decade. I started doing everything I knew to do—drinking loads of green juice, downing spirulina, meditating and walking outdoors as much as possible. I had read of people whose cancers had spontaneously gone away when they were able to get to the emotional root of the issue and energetically fix the problem.

At that moment in my life, of these tools, I believed in energy medicine the most. So after leaving the hospital, I beelined to both my acupuncturist and my energy psychotherapist during my one day of medical freedom.

⁙

The principle governing all energy techniques is that *everything* is energy, and many of the symptoms we experience are a result of the disruption of these invisible streams and sources. The body is alive through electric, electromagnetic, and more subtle energies that can be shifted with various modalities. In Traditional Chinese Medicine, which is where we get acupuncture and acupressure, energy runs through lines in the body called meridians that are associated with different organs and other body systems. A skilled acupuncturist, which I was fortunate enough to have, uses thin needles at different points on these meridians to bring the body back into harmony. I had begun seeing an acupuncturist when I was 24—amid intense panic attacks—and had found it highly effective for my anxiety and insomnia. At that point, I still saw an acupuncturist periodically for a tune-up or more regularly during times of stress.

Acupuncture is just one form of energy medicine, and the meridian system just one of many energetic systems in and around the body. The other practitioner I saw used a system of tapping on my back while I spoke aloud the challenges I was facing, helping to move me into a more peaceful and accepting state of being. This was a method she had developed herself called the Energetic Repatterning Technique.[3] I also used the Emotional Freedom Technique (widely known as *tapping*) for self-care when I was unable to visit my practitioner, which is based on similar concepts.

Both of these people were amazing at helping me shift energy, but I only got in a few sessions before having to rely on tools that I could use on my own. Just a few weeks after my diagnosis, the pandemic shut the world down and I no longer had access to these practitioners. Fortunately, I had been learning ways to work with energy independently, most recently through Eden Energy Medicine (EEM). Donna Eden's book *Energy Medicine: Balancing Your Body's Energies for Optimal Health, Joy, and Vitality* had already become a well-loved and worn book on my shelf. I would turn to it often during my course of treatment. I used many of her resources—before, during, and after chemotherapy—and they always helped me feel stronger and more vibrant in the face of the poison. Energy work I could do myself became vitally important, so EEM along with acupressure and tapping became staples in my life during treatment. Though I missed my practitioners, it was empowering to have resources I could work with that did not require travel time and money.

But later in the year when the pandemic regulations loosened, I found myself anxiously seeking more and more practitioners for help. In my state of stress and concern, I bounced around trying different methods. These sessions grew expensive and tiring. I believe one practitioner, with one method, seen weekly or every other week—along with regular self-care—would have been more harmonious for me. I realized in my recovery years that all of my appointments were actually perpetuating my state of disempowerment. I fell into a cycle of thinking I needed to go see healers in order to be okay. If going to appointments becomes stressful for any reason, back off and keep it simple—use some self-care resources and call it a day.

I highly recommend experimenting with energy medicine if you are going through chemotherapy. Whether it is acupuncture, acupressure, EEM, tapping or sound healing (among many others), these are non-invasive approaches with no possibility of interacting negatively with the conventional treatment. In my experience, energy work helps the body cope with side effects and release what is stuck. Chemotherapy and energy medicine cooperate well with one another.

Everything we do and experience—the words we speak, the thoughts we think, anything we put into our bodies, the people around us, and the larger cosmic structures and systems—all affect the energies in and around our bodies. Whether it is meditation and prayer, nutrition and plant medicine, sound and frequency, color or laughter or play—it is *all* energy medicine. Even chemotherapy itself has energetic properties. But some modalities more directly approach the invisible energy systems: the meridians, the chakras, other circuits and rhythms in the body, and the biofield around the body that is part of the system, too. I am choosing to differentiate *energy medicine* in this chapter to acknowledge that the techniques I speak of come from systems that focus on actively shifting the subtle energies.

To work with the energy systems is to become conscious of our bodies in new ways. This was imperative for me during chemotherapy. Sometimes the chemo would make me feel disconnected from my own experience, confused and tense. When I was able to tap into the invisible happenings within and around me, I experienced a more harmonious existence with my treatment. This would become a significant concept: no matter what was going on with my treatment, no matter what toxins were pumped into my system, it was possible to be in harmony with these medicines.

Energy medicine helped me cultivate that harmony. The chemo and the energy medicine weren't competing systems; they were both healers who helped one another. Working with energy gave me a sense of fluidity and peace, movement and brightness—even in the face of fear, uncertainty, and poison. It brought my discomfort level down a notch or two, and it strengthened my body and my spirit. I did not make it through my treatment in record time, but I believe these resources did help me get through it with more ease.

Energy

Tapping

Tapping is a simple yet powerful technique that you can work with any time there is a block that is keeping you from releasing the tension of negative emotion. It uses points on the meridian system, like acupressure and acupuncture. The basics of tapping are as follows:

1. Identify an issue or emotion that is challenging you. Rate the intensity of the issue on a scale from 0 to 10.

2. Acknowledge this challenge, while accepting yourself fully. Create a statement along these lines: "Even though I am feeling and/or experiencing _____, I deeply and completely accept myself."

3. Follow the tapping sequence on the chart below. Tap the twelve tapping points while focusing on the issue and speaking out loud the statement in step 2. As you tap, begin to speak the detail of the feeling or experience. Tap in the order found in the next page for 1-2 rounds in this manner. Then move your speech toward the release of this experience or feeling for 1-2 rounds. Finally, tap 1-2 rounds while you speak a positive hope: what would it be like if this emotion or experience were accepted and moved through the body and the energetic system?

4. Rate the intensity of the issue again on a scale from 0 to 10. If the intensity is still high, do more rounds of tapping as needed.

Chapter Resources

These are the tapping points:

Top of the head (GV20)

The inside end of the eyebrow (B2)

Side of the eye (GB1)

Under the eye (St 1)

Under the nose (GV26)

Under the lip (CV24)

Collar bone points (K27)

Middle of the chest (CV17)

Under the arms (Sp 21)

Side of the leg (GB 32)

Side of the hand (SI 3)

The ridge beneath the ring and little finger (TW 3)

Chapter Resources

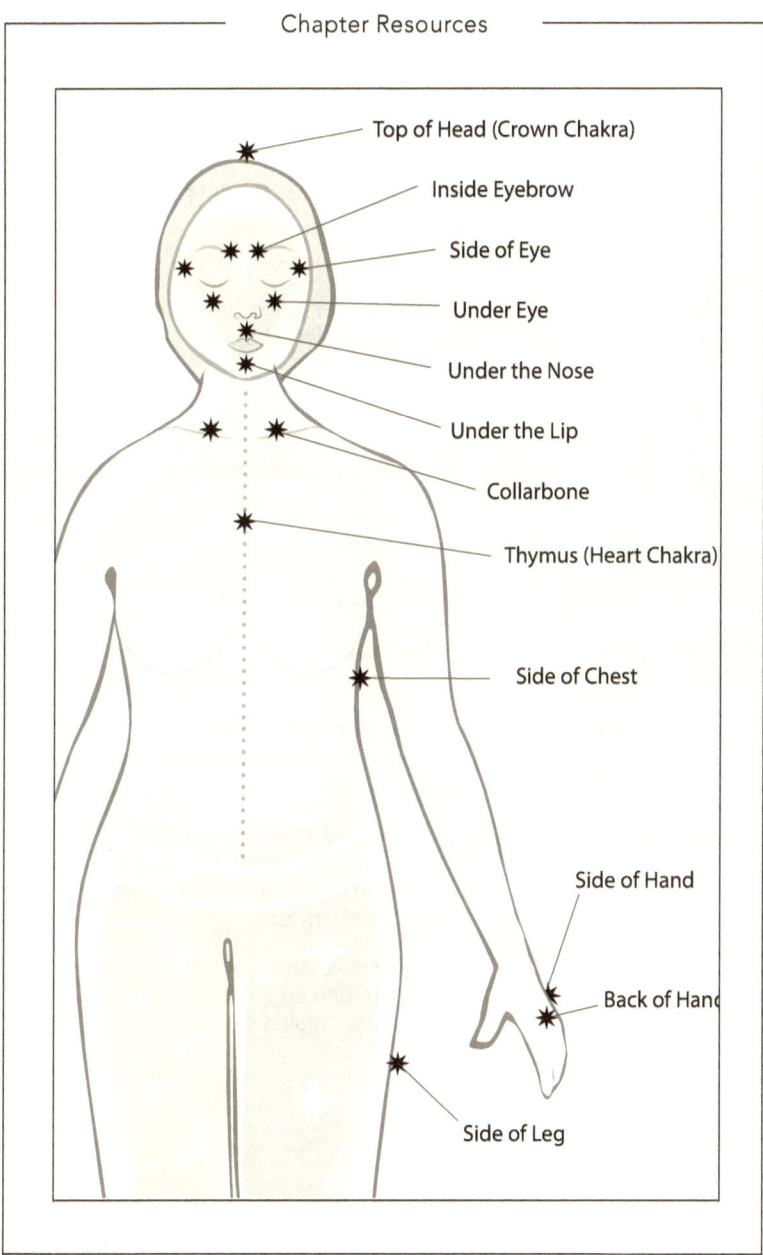

Top of Head (Crown Chakra)

Inside Eyebrow

Side of Eye

Under Eye

Under the Nose

Under the Lip

Collarbone

Thymus (Heart Chakra)

Side of Chest

Side of Hand

Back of Hand

Side of Leg

Chapter Resources

Acupressure Points[4]

You can hold, rub or lightly thump acupressure points. Here are a few of my favorites:

Sea of Tranquility (CV 17) — On the center of the breastbone, three thumb-lengths up from the base.

Gates of Consciousness (GB 20) — Two points that are below the base of the skull, in the hollow between the neck muscles, two or three inches apart.

Inner Gate (P6) — In the middle of the inner forearm, 2.5 finger-widths from the crease of the wrist.

Spirit Gate (H7) — At the crease of the wrist on the pinky finger side of the forearm.

Heavenly Pillar (B 10) — Half an inch below the base of the skull, on the muscles that are half an inch away from the spine.

Letting Go (Lu 1) — On the upper chest near the shoulders, four finger-widths upward from the armpit, and one finger-width inward.

Three Mile Point (St 36) — Four finger-widths below the kneecap, one finger-width toward the outside of the shinbone.

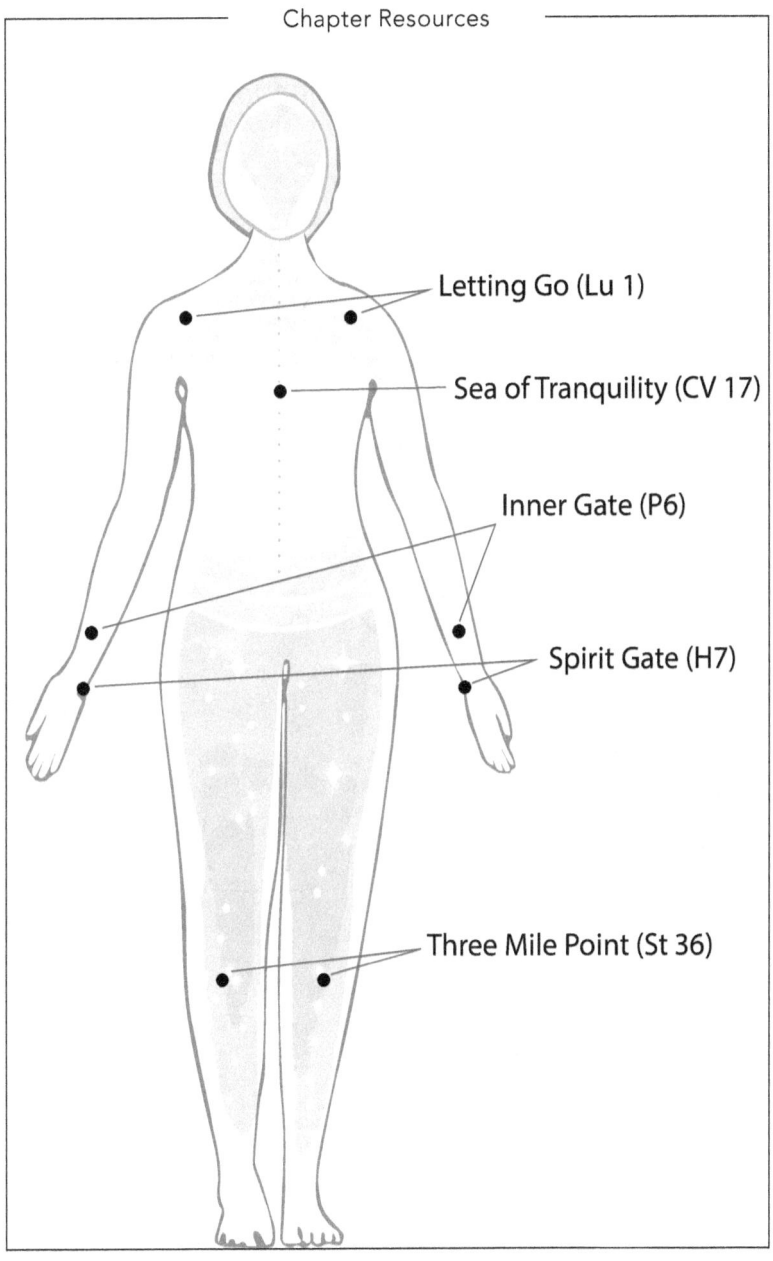

Chapter Resources

Letting Go (Lu 1)

Sea of Tranquility (CV 17)

Inner Gate (P6)

Spirit Gate (H7)

Three Mile Point (St 36)

Chapter Resources

Gates of Consciousness (GB 20)

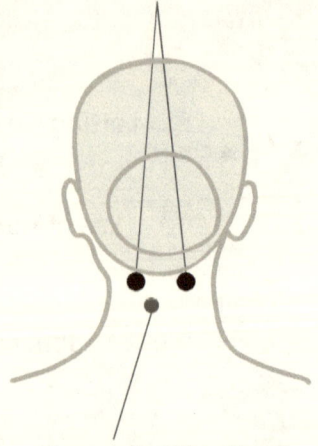

Heavenly Pillar (B 10)

EEM Daily Energy Routine

This is a simple series I used before, during, and after chemotherapy and tuned into my intuition for guidance as to how much and which techniques felt the best. *If you search YouTube you can find several instructional videos.*

Restoration

I arrived at Duke Cancer Center for my first inpatient infusion two nights after being released from the hospital. I walked through the electronic, sliding doors and checked in for my labs on the first floor. They drew blood; I chitchatted with the nurse. The cancer center is a friendly place. There are big windows and a lot of light, and the facility feels newer and more open than the hospital.

They sent me upstairs to the clinic by way of the elevator. We waited for the lab results and for the drugs to be ordered. I sat nervously in the big waiting room with all of the other cancer patients. I was one of them now.

A clinic nurse brought me back to an infusion room, and I was immediately given some good news: my hCG level had dropped miraculously from 655,000 (this number is in IU/L, but I am not going to specify going forward) all the way down to 1061 after my first chemotherapy treatment. This was a huge and unexpected drop. Whew, how I had needed some good news. The goal for hCG—my cancer marker—was 1.2. After I reached 1.2, there would be a bonus round or two of chemotherapy. I was really on my way. I felt such a relief and chalked it up to the wellness living resources that I was utilizing with vigor.

With this information, the second induction round of chemotherapy was made a little bit easier. I received it and went on my merry way back home to the farmhouse.

But when I arrived home, the high of the good news began to wear off. My body was feeling very weak, which I did not like to admit.

I went out for a barefoot walk on our land. I didn't make it far before I had to stop and catch my breath. On the ground I sat, gazing at the clouds, trying to understand what was happening. I sank hard from my hopeful state, feeling disoriented by how different my life was now, suddenly. I became angry, and the anger of the whole situation stayed with me for a long time. I now had to live in this alternate medical system prison universe that no one else around me had to live in, and I felt disempowered and stuck. *Why was my body sick?* I felt like I had been at war with my body for decades: through medical trauma, struggling with my appearance, or anxiety and panic. The experience of powerlessness over my own body was not new. I was also angry that I had been living the healthiest life I knew to live, and it wasn't enough. I was 35, and I had cancer. This truth was unfathomable to me. Coming to terms with it would take a long time.

It was March now, and warm spring air was arriving. I continued to sit there on the earth for a long time, just kind of...stunned. I touched my hair, knowing my long locks would be gone in a week or two. I wanted to be a person who didn't care about whether she had hair or not. But I did care. I knew I would not look like myself without hair.

The isolation of this medical experience was peculiar: on one hand, there were often many people around me. I was lucky enough to have a loving family there who would rub my feet and cook for me. They would care for my children; they would listen to my stress. But on the other hand, no one else near me had this poison in their body. It was simply true that for the next year I would live in a world that was not the same one my caregivers lived in. My physical, emotional, and spiritual experiences were drastically different. Communication and real understanding were not quite possible.

Parenting during this illness was another layer to confront. My relationship with motherhood was complicated. My cancer came directly from my pregnancy—my body was filled with tumors made up of the pregnancy hormone. I had been struggling so much with parenting young children, so I couldn't help but see this illness as tied in some way to my experience of smotherhood. My mind turned often to that question: *Would motherhood kill me, too?*

I truly wanted to be a better mother. I wanted to experience that joy of parenting that it seemed like others experienced. I wanted to feel strong and to feel connected to my children, to be a solid role model for my daughters, to help them learn and grow. Elsie and Beatrice deserved this. Yet, I always felt like I was coming up short.

I lay on the ground—smashed down and broken to pieces, desperately in need of restoration.

⌒◌⌒

Back in 2005, I took an undergraduate class called Comparing Contemplative Traditions. I was a mathematics major, so it wasn't an ordinary choice for me. But I found myself drawn to these practices of contemplation and meditation, of finding slowness in a life of overwhelming stimuli. And God. I thought much about God. My church upbringing planted a seed of interest in the Divine, but it would take a long time for me to find a form of spirituality that felt authentic to me. It is still a work in progress, and will likely always ebb and flow as life continues.

In this class, we taste-tested a variety of contemplative practices from various spiritual and philosophical systems. There was one practice that really drew me in: *yoga nidra*—the practice of deep rest or *yogic sleep*. It is an ancient resource that has been developed over time, and used with great success to rest the physical body and restore the spirit. It is a guided meditation, but it is not your average guided meditation. It does something truly different than any other kind of guided meditation I have encountered—and I have encountered many. It occupies the mind through verbal instruction, leads you into your body, and encourages the release of tension and the restoration of the spiritual self. In yoga nidra, you lie down and go through a rotation of consciousness, awareness of breath, experience of sensation, and visualization through the body that triggers a deeply restful state. In this space, we can work through unconscious patterns and spiritual blockages. The folklore says that an hour of yoga nidra is equal to the rest of a three-hour nap. It is truly an experience of physical, mental, and spiritual restoration when practiced regularly.

I believe that our physical bodies are linked to our emotions and our spiritual existence. Humans are multi-faceted beings. So I knew that the cancer in my body was not an isolated physical experience; it was related to my mind and to my spirit, too. This is not meant to say that I believe we cause our cancer, or that if we have incurable cancer it is somehow our fault—but that we must work with each and every layer of the experience when going through a challenging situation. My relationship with motherhood was something I had to work with while going through this illness. There were also other layers that I had to engage—my environment, my relationships, my ancestral history, and my sense of self and of communal belonging.

The year of treatment forced me to face myself. I had to dig in and accept what was happening in me on these deeper levels. This was one of the gifts of the experience, and one of the most laborious parts. I committed to journaling, to noticing what was going on within all of the parts of my being. I examined my own life, raised questions, and came to terms with aspects of myself that had been hidden or shoved away. It was often lonely, yet this cocoon was the space of transformation.

I already knew that one of the challenging patterns I needed to break was the inability to rest. This was tied to motherhood as well as the pressure that I had put on myself since I was a child. Even when people gave me the space to rest, I was not able. I did not feel allowed on a deeper, spiritual level. I slept terribly and was constantly buzzing with ideas and information. I know that I am not the only one in our society who feels that rest is not permissible. We are going, moving, working, taking in information all the time. We are told we must be constantly productive and that this is where our value lies. The average person does not have time for restoration.

Cancer forced rest on me in a way that I did not care for. I found myself alone, being told to *go rest*, but not really wanting to do this. Allowing rest felt like succumbing to the illness, and when I rested too much, I felt myself snowball into an incapacitated childlike state. Balance is always key.

When going through chemotherapy, movement, purpose and productivity are quite important. Being with people and tending to regular activities as much as possible can help tremendously. And so does deep, restorative rest. I knew that I would need to rest in a different way—to go to that cocoon of yogic sleep in order to heal.

Restoration is different from lounging. Lounging—scrolling, watching TV, eating snacks on the couch—is its own (sometimes enjoyable) thing. But real rest in the body and the spirit doesn't happen in that place. I needed the kind of rest that would give my body the space and capacity to heal. To do this, I re-committed to my yoga nidra practice, and it was truly one of my most potent resources through my year of chemotherapy. The recordings I found on the internet weren't cutting it anymore, so I began writing and recording my own yoga nidra sessions. These proved incredibly useful for my year in treatment.

Almost every day, I practiced for 30-45 minutes by listening to the audio that guided me into a liminal state of consciousness—not asleep, not awake. I crawled into the safe space of rest and healing and allowed my body and spirit to find stillness. In this state, energy shifted and re-patterned, and my mind became quiet as the busyness fell away. Subtle transformations occurred each time I practiced.

I always felt rejuvenated after these sessions, able to think more clearly, sleep better, and have a more peaceful and hopeful outlook. I cannot overstate how powerful this resource is for anyone going through chemotherapy—or any challenging life experience, for that matter. Regular practice brings restoration. I highly recommend this as a simple yet profound method for coming into a state of complete rest, awareness of self, and spiritual transformation.

Restoration

Basic Yoga Nidra

Record this for yourself or have another speak it for you:

(Intention)

Begin with a few minutes of silence as you settle into a comfortable position lying on your back. You may want a thin pillow under your head, a bolster or pillow underneath your knees, and/or an eye pillow.

As your body begins to settle, close your eyes in preparation for engaging this practice. Set your attention free to wander through the senses. Note the sounds around you in the room, the images and thoughts that are passing through your mind in this moment, and the feeling of your body. As you do this, please allow my words to become your words as we enter into this meditative journey together.

I invite you to be open to the stillness and awareness of the bright, stable light within you. Come to the knowledge that the core of your being is unchanging. With this realization, you can face any challenge you are met with in this life.

Affirm the following to yourself as you enter the practice of yoga nidra:

> *I am awake.*

> *I am aware.*

> *I am open to experiencing rest and my unchanging, deepest Self.*

Chapter Resources

Now feel and affirm this resolve as you quietly repeat these affirmations a couple more times to yourself.

> *I am awake. I am aware. I am open to experiencing rest and my unchanging, deepest Self.*

(Rotation of Consciousness)

Be aware of your entire body. Feel the body as radiant.

Be aware of the mouth. Feel the sensations in the tongue and mouth. In the teeth and the insides of your cheeks.

Feel the inside of the right ear. The outer form of the right ear.

Feel the inside of the left ear. The outer form of the left ear.

Feel the right cheek. Left cheek. Both cheeks.

The nose. Feel the sensation of breath as it passes in and out through the nostrils.

Feel the right eye. Left eye. Both eyes. Space between the eyes.

The forehead. The scalp. Back of the head. Back of the neck.

Come back to the sensations in both eyes. Follow the sensation of the eyes all the way to the inside the of head. To the inner contents of the brain. The right side of the brain. The left side of the brain. The entire head.

Mouth, ears, nose, scalp. Inside of the head. The entire head as radiant warm light.

The throat.

Chapter Resources

Right shoulder. Right elbow. Right wrist. Right thumb. Second finger, middle finger, ring finger, pinky finger. Right wrist, right elbow, right shoulder.

Left shoulder. Left elbow. Left wrist. Left thumb. Second finger, middle finger, ring finger, pinky finger. Left wrist, left elbow, left shoulder.

Be aware of both arms at the same time. Be aware of both palms of the hands. Hands as warm, radiant light.

Both arms at the same time. The throat. The chest. Upper back. Abdomen. Lower back. Sides of the abdomen. The entire abdomen as warm radiant light.

Both hips.

Right hip. Right knee, right ankle, right foot. Big toe, second toe, third toe, fourth toe, fifth toe. Right foot, right ankle, right knee, right hip.

Left hip. Left knee, left ankle, left foot. Big toe, second toe, third toe, fourth toe, fifth toe. Left foot, left ankle, left knee, left hip.

Both hips as radiant warm light.

Both legs as radiant warm light.

And now experience the whole body as radiant, warm light.

Bathe in this light, feeling grounded, relaxed, warm, and safe.

Chapter Resources

(The Breath)

Now notice the body itself breathing. Notice the inhale and the exhale—slow and steady.

Feel the breath enter your feet on your inhale. Breath flowing up both legs, through your hips and abdomen, through your heart, throat, and to the top of your head. Exhale the breath down your shoulders, down your arms, and out your fingertips.

Continue in this rhythmic sort of breathing. Slow, deep inhale through your feet and all the way up your body. Slow, deep exhale down your arms and out your fingertips. Each time you transition between inhale and exhale, exhale and inhale, experience a moment of stillness in the body.

Now feel the breath as warm light. As you inhale, it fills your entire being with bright, warm light. This loving light reaches each cell of your body, nourishing your entire being. And as you exhale, the light stays within you, and you exhale love and compassion out into the world with ease. Continue to feel the breath as warm, loving light.

(Awareness of Sensation)

Draw your attention to a place in your body that feels heavy. Then feel heavy in every part of your body. Feel so heavy that you are sinking. Sinking slowly into the ground beneath you. Feel heavy. Heavy. *Heavy.*

Draw your attention to a place in your body that feels lightness, weightlessness. Then feel lightness in every part of your body. Your body is so light that it seems to be floating. Floating. *Floating.*

Draw your attention to a place in your body that feels cold. Then feel cold throughout your entire body. Cold all over, like winter in a snowstorm. Cold like winter. *Cold.*

Draw your attention to a place in your body that feels warm. Then feel warm throughout your entire body. Warm all over, like hot summer sun. Warm like hot summer sun. *Warm.*

Draw your attention to a memory of pain. Any type of pain you have experienced in your life. Feel it in your body now. Feel the pain in your whole body. *Pain.*

Draw your attention to a memory of joy. Any type of joy you have experienced in your life. Feel this memory in your body—in every cell of your being. Feel the brightness of this joy radiating, pulsing through you vividly. *Joy.*

(Inner Space)

Move past any thought space and concentrate only on the space in front of your closed eyes. See in front of you infinite, expansive space. Concentrate only on this dark space that extends far out beyond perception. Allow, then, anything within this space to manifest—anything that might arise. Become aware but not attached to that which is there.

(Visualization)

Imagine that you are outside in the dark of early morning. Sunrise will come soon, but for now, you feel the stillness, the quiet of the night. You are walking, slowly but in strength,

Chapter Resources

toward a mountain that lies in the distance ahead of you. You know it is there, but it is not yet in view. You are all alone.

You continue walking toward the mountain, which is in the east where the sun will show itself when the time comes. You pause and scan the sky all around you, noticing a few twinkling stars and a crescent moon sitting low. Toward the west is a small town in a valley behind you, and you feel the energy of people beginning to wake. You walk along a winding path, and it becomes rocky and slightly treacherous at different points. You climb over large rocks and traverse dirt bridges over deep valleys. You continue along the winding path until you come to a place where you can clearly see the bottom of the mountain up ahead. It is a large mountain with a snow-covered peak, and though it is still dark, you begin to climb. You know in your being that there is something beautiful at the top. You climb and climb, and the wind blows, and it becomes colder and colder.

You walk and walk, and you finally reach where the rock turns to snow-covered ground, near the top. The ice crunches beneath your feet. For a moment, you are not sure you will make it to the top, but you gather the courage to continue just as you begin to see the colors of sunrise in the sky. The sun has not yet appeared, but your spirit is filled with pink, yellow, and purple hues as you keep going.

You reach the very top of the mountain just as the sun shows itself as a bright, radiant ball of light. You stand there experiencing this miracle, the scattering of the light and the illumination of the earth. A brand-new day. You sit down and breathe this place in deeply. This majestic experience of bright, new life. Of vast, expansive beauty. Miraculous regeneration and renewal. Flow into this experience with your entire self.

Chapter Resources

(Inner Space)

Now move back into your vast, dark inner space in front of your closed eyes. See in front of you infinite, expansive space. Concentrate only on this dark space that extends far out beyond perception. Allow, then, anything within this space to manifest—anything that might arise. Become aware but not attached to that which is there.

(Resolve)

Return now to your intention for this practice: *I am awake, I am aware, I am open to experiencing rest and my unchanging, deepest Self.*

(Return to Daily Life)

Begin to become aware of the present moment.

Become aware of your breathing.

Become aware of your body—Your arms and legs.

Feel the surface beneath you.

Become aware of the space around you—the environment near your body.

You hear sounds near to you. Then your awareness expands, and you experience your wider present environment. Lie quietly for a few moments.

Begin to move your body. First your fingers and toes.

When you are ready, stretch a little bit. Take your time.

Chapter Resources

When you are sure that you are awake and present, sit up slowly and take a few breaths with your eyes closed.

Open your eyes to a bright journey head.[5]

The Brightest Self

It was Saturday morning, almost two weeks since my diagnosis—March 7th, to be exact. I lay in bed at the farmhouse until late morning, but then experienced a burst of fresh energy. I got out of bed, feeling like I might be capable of spending some time with my children. I had been missing them so much. The girls were cuddled on the couch enjoying Daniel Tiger in the living room. I nestled in between those two little humans and felt some of that motherhood joy that was hard to come by lately. I would get to snuggle with them today, and I was so grateful.

For ten whole minutes, I cherished that couch cuddle—but then I started to cough. This was a wet cough; I could feel it. Those were the worst kind. I looked into my hands and saw that there was more blood than there had been lately. I got up bewildered, went to the bathroom for tissues, and called the doctor. I needed to get to the emergency room, and I did not want the girls to see the blood. So I slipped out quietly without saying goodbye, my heart breaking, and found my way back to the hospital.

⌒∞⌒

I sat on the edge of a patient table in the ER, waiting for blood test and CT scan results.

Click, click, click. Dr. Davidson appeared in front of me. She had results and I could tell they were not of the happy sort. She began with the first piece of confusing news: my hCG level was back up to over 489,000. The other thing that was going on was that I had a pulmonary embolism—a blood clot in my lungs. She thought this was likely a result of the chemotherapy shaking things up.

She told me that she would have to put me in the ICU.

The ICU. *This cannot be good.* I sank in fear and defeat and my mind wandered to my little girls sitting on the couch. Daniel Tiger was over by now—*where did they think I had gone? Were they scared, too?* Or was I such a mother failure that my presence didn't actually matter to them anyway?

When I landed in the ER, there was a part of me that truly believed they were going to tell me I did not have cancer anymore and that this coughing incident was just the last of it moving out of my system. It was Robert's birthday, after all—perhaps some ancestor magic would come through.

But that was not the case. It was kind of...the opposite. This healing would take much longer than expected. My sometimes-evangelical belief in the system of wellness living shattered that day. I realized then that this was going to be more complicated. It would take years to accept how many layers there were to this illness. The healing would require me to traverse them, to access and work in the depths of my spirit in new ways. In the coming year, I would learn to unite and balance Western medicine with wellness living. I would utilize a truly integrated approach—and my time in the ICU was the beginning of this integration.

Another doctor entered the room where I sat with Dr. Davidson and probably with Matt. Dr. Davidson introduced him as Dr. Nathaniel Harris. He was the ICU doctor, so he would be medically in charge during my stay.

Dr. Harris was friendly, but I don't clearly remember what he looked like. I think he was kind of short. Maybe a little goofy. On the younger end? He reassured me that a stay in the ICU was more preventive than anything else. Pulmonary embolisms can be unpredictable, and we want to be prepared. If something happens, then everything needed would be at our disposal, so the ICU was the right place for me.

But I was intensely scared. My memory floated to the last time I had been in the ICU.

It was the middle of the night, and I was interning as a hospital chaplain at Duke in 2012. I was called from the tiny windowless cell where the chaplain on-call slept. I was probably not sleeping but more likely eating questionable food from the cafeteria and watching *How I Met Your Mother* on my computer.

A woman was dying and had requested the chaplain. That was me. I was 27 years old then, the summer before my last year of divinity school. I was required to wear a white coat—the short kind that the medical interns wear. I put it on—it always felt awkward, like I was playing doctor—and walked to the middle of the main hospital where the ICU was. There were no windows there, either.

No windows, but about twenty people gathered around the dying matriarch of their family. They were a Black family, and I was a young little white girl. I walked up to this big group and hesitantly tapped someone on the shoulder who was much taller than me.

"Um, hi...I'm Hannah...I'm the...chaplain." I told this person meekly. I did not feel that I was the right person for this job. I wasn't even a real chaplain.

"Pastor! You're here, that's great." And everyone in the circle looked at me expectantly. I wasn't going to correct them that I was not a pastor, not yet, probably not ever.

They were looking for something in this moment—their mother was dying. *Oh dear Jesus, why me?* I stood silently. *A bible verse? Words of encouragement? What were they looking for? What do they need?* We didn't know one another at all. I couldn't possibly be of help.

I stood there blankly for what felt like an hour. Then I finally took a deep breath and spoke the first thing that came to me: "Do you want to sing?" I asked with confident hesitation.

The idea was well-received. Whew. They did want to sing. What song would it be? I don't remember now, but the family found an old gospel tune, nameless in my memory.

The ICU was filled with song. Maybe it woke some people up—singing does seem to have that effect. I did not know the song, so I didn't sing, but my spirit was filled. The song of humans together does something to me that nothing else does. I melded with my surroundings into a place of bliss and connection—right on the ledge of happy tears.

The memory I had of the ICU was beautiful, but it was also terrifying. The ICU was where people were sent when they were dying, or at least when that was a possibility. I did not want to go there. I thought again of my little girls back home. *Elsie and Bea, Elsie and Bea, Elsie and Bea.* Oh, my stomach churned.

Someone wheeled me into my ICU room. I was feeling confused and powerless again. This place was different from the ICU room I had been in before. It was in a brand new wing of the hospital, and it was spacious with a big window. There were a lot more machines here than in a regular hospital room, and a couch that folded down into a twin-sized bed. This would be my home for the next seven days.

There were often people in and out. Family members and friends took turns staying with me when they could. Nurses flitted around, doctors and medical students came in. At one point, a whole big medical team filled the room, interested in my case of this rare cancer.

Over the course of this stay in the ICU, the world would shut down with the pandemic, and this was the last time all of these extra people were allowed with me in the hospital.

In the ICU, it is standard to always have an IV hook-up in both arms. This was precautionary—if an emergency arose, it could save my life to be able to receive two medicines simultaneously. So I had a needle stuck in both sides. Through one, I received a high-dose antibiotic; in the other, I received nothing. I hadn't taken an antibiotic in 15 years—it was not part of wellness living, after all. I didn't care anymore, I just wanted to get through this.

During the initial days there, I was on strict no-food orders, with as little liquid as possible—just in case. I grew tired of this very quickly. I was hungry and thirsty and mad. I was coughing blood, yet I felt strangely good. A nurse would come in and check my IVs every once in a while to make sure they were still working, but at some point, one of them stalled. And so began the adventure of trying to get a working IV into my second arm while I was fasting and already a *hard stick*. My veins are small, and it was challenging to find one even when I was well-hydrated.

Several different people came in to try and get a needle in. They poked and prodded and used ultrasound and a warm compress. Over and over. My arm was exhausted and in pain. I flashed back to that time when I was nineteen, bleeding out my throat, jabbed and scraped in my arms as they looked for a proper vein. *Could we just take a break?* I begged. Yes, but they would be back.

I took a breath. Had a little cry. The arm digging was really miserable for me.

It wasn't long before Dr. Harris walked in to check on me. He wasn't a *clicker*, but he strode in with clear confidence.

"How are we doing?" He asked, kind of happy-like.

"We are not doing well." I answer, definitely unhappy-like. "I'm starving and they won't let me eat, I'm thirsty and they will only let me suck on ice, they have been digging in my arm for like an hour and why do I even need a second IV? And I'm in the ICU! Why am I here? I don't need to be here. So...I don't know...I guess I'm fine. *Fine!* Super wonderful!" I think Dr. Harris laughed at my outburst.

"What's funny?! What am I supposed to do here?"

Dr. Harris got kind of quiet, and I could tell he was trying to decide whether or not to say something.

"Okay, look, I can't tell you what to do. But I can tell you what I would do if I were you."

"Please, yes, tell me."

"I would order a hamburger and fries, and I would eat it all. And maybe I'd order a coke, too—and slurp that thing down."

"Seriously?"

"Yep. And I would tell them that I don't want a second IV because it's my body and I'm a grown-ass woman and I get to decide what happens to it."

"*Seriously?!?*"

"That's just what I would do. You do whatever you want to do. You're the grown-ass woman." And he gave me a wry smile and confidently strode out of the room.

⚬◦∞◦⚬

A grown-ass woman? These words felt foreign to me. I am sure that somewhere along the way someone had told me that I was a grown-up, that my body belonged to me. But the words hadn't matched my experience, so there was dissonance and confusion in me when Dr. Harris said it. I did not feel like a grown-ass woman.

As usual, there are so many layers. I struggled to feel like an adult because I had never lived into my idea of what an adult was. These ideas came from my culture, from my family, and from my own internal system. An adult is a person who makes money and does not need the financial assistance of anyone else. An adult does not look like a high schooler. An adult takes care of the people around her with all that she has and is very happy to do this. That's basically it. These were the messages I had internalized and I had never met these expectations. *Grown-ass woman?* I didn't think so. (Of course I had been sorely misinformed, for a grown-ass woman is simply one who operates out of self-respect.)

I had been dragging along for years, feeling more or less like a failure of a human, a kid who couldn't pull it together. We had moved to a farm that I didn't have the energy to care for, I felt myself a negligent and frustrating partner, and generally a bad parent. Grown-ups were able to do all these things with ease and flow. I was not. People had to help me—financially, emotionally, and now physically—and adults aren't supposed to need help.

And my body, did it belong to me? I wasn't sure. Through natural child birthing I had felt empowered, in a way, to advocate for myself in the medical system. In school I had studied the history of women's rights and body autonomy. But it still felt like there was a threshold, an upper limit, to how much autonomy I might actually exercise.

The medical system was one layer. There were also cultural and religious layers. Who owned my body? Who had that power? I was not sure of the answer, but it felt like my body belonged to a good many other people who were not me.

In this simple conversation, Dr. Harris—unassuming young white man, though obviously incredibly brilliant—offered me an empowering possibility. He managed to stir a question in my soul: *why did I feel so childlike, and not in a good way?* Unable to speak my truth or stand up for myself. Mushy, even. It was no one's fault, really; it was just how life had been set up. Dr. Harris handed me some power that I desperately needed. Power to stand strong in myself, to be a grown-ass woman who owns her own body.

A few days later, I perked up. I was still in the ICU, but it was only because there was not a free bed in the main hospital. I started to enjoy (as much as a person might enjoy) the big room with the window and space to move around. I sat on the window sill and gazed out at Durham—this little city I had spent seven years living in. What an experience, to be back in this capacity.

I was able to convince the nurse to walk with me through the maze-like halls and downstairs to meet my children outside for a quick *hello*. They were not allowed in the ICU. It was brief, but lifted my spirits to see them looking happy. They were getting to spend a lot of time with their grandmother—my mother, their *Esa* (she spells it this way and pronounces it ee-sah)—and they all enjoyed being together. Any moments I got to see them in this acute phase of treatment brought warmth to my whole self. Slowly, I could feel the growth of the mother in me that somehow hadn't found her way yet.

We arrived back in the ICU room, and I stood talking with the nurse who had walked me through the hospital. He was a traveling nurse on assignment here for just a few weeks.

"Have you ever had an ICU patient walk out of the room?" I asked.

"Hmm, no, I don't think I have."

"Have you ever had an ICU patient do...this?" And I did a little dance.

"No. Definitely not."

I was annoyingly smug, yet also feeling and expressing a glimpse of something brighter in myself. I hadn't expected to find it in the ICU.

There was a dormant empowered Self eager to break free. A wise being deep within me that had been struggling to speak, to liberate, to be. Some would call this the Higher Self or the Wise Self—I like to call her the Brightest Self. She is that core of my being who is strong, who can tap into her intuition with ease, who stands up for herself in word and action without tearing others down. She is illuminated and sparkly. We all have a Brightest Self.

Following my intuition—developing the part of myself that can listen deeply within and outside of me—became an important part of this journey. Standing in my power meant being able to slow down and sense what was going to benefit my body. Going through this toxic process allowed me to enter into my intuition more fully, resisting my typical desire to please those around me and follow their guidelines without question. There is something about an extreme event that opens us up to new insight. I learned to listen more sincerely to my intuition through writing, sound, and meditation.

The ability to listen to and follow your intuition will be a game changer—whether it is about treatment or any of the challenging decisions that will arise during your oncology experience. This fact is well-documented in Kelly A. Turner's book *Radical Remission: Surviving Cancer Against All Odds*.[6] This book is also a wonderful resource that I had read earlier in life and re-visited numerous times during my treatment.

A symbol began to form in my vision, and I saw my Brightest Self as a big, strong tree—a Mother Tree. Deep roots, nourished foliage, sturdy and upright. She breathes in a rhythm that feeds the environment around her. She is even able to cleanse the air of toxins as she creates new oxygen. She dances with the wind.

When I struggled that year to feel strong, I looked to the trees. I still do. I believe the trees can help us all tap into our powerful, Brightest Selves. I also know that there may be a unique image that arrives in you to help you know and be this Self. Embracing your power and developing your intuition are imperative for healing, whatever it is that must heal. When going through a toxic experience like chemotherapy, stand tall in that power, speak up for yourself, and know that within you resides your Brightest Self that is rooted into the earth and growing toward the light.

The Brightest Self

Find Your Voice

Look for opportunities to speak, to sing, and to make sounds. These ways of expressing the literal voice help to nurture the more subtle voices that must find their place in order for the Brightest Self to flourish.

Standing Tree Meditation

Ideally, this is done outside and barefoot, but use whatever environment is available. You can definitely do it in the treatment room! Use this simple meditation when you need a quick dose of your strong, Brightest Self.

Stand if you are able.

Shake out your legs and arms, and move around a little bit, releasing any obvious tension from the body.

Let go with three big sighs, allowing yourself to make whatever sounds come out of your body.

Then come into stillness. Stand balanced and steady on the ground. Breathe slowly and deeply in and out of your nose.

Bring your attention to your feet and imagine yourself with roots growing from the bottom of your feet. The roots are strong and healthy, slowly seeping into the soil. They are solid and have formed in exactly the place where they need to be. Breathe into these roots.

Chapter Resources

Moving upward, feel your legs and your core as the tree's trunk. One strong, upright form with many layers. The outside is firm bark, a strong but kind boundary. Inside are circles upon circles. The innermost layer has been there the longest, and you experience the bright, wise core that lies deep within. Breathe deeply into this sturdy trunk.

Deep roots, strong trunk.

Now experience your upper body—chest, arms, head—as branches. Extending outward and upward. Toward sky and air and brightness. Always growing a little bit at a time, expanding but still rooted and strong. You may feel your arms floating upward, a smile might form on your face.

Stand as the wise, adult tree and breathe into this experience for as long as you would like.

Find Your Own Brightest Self Image

There are many ways you might find an image that works for you to bring out your Brightest Self. Stream of consciousness writing, sound, movement, meditation, and visual art can all be powerful resources for the expression of this image. Choose a modality and hold this question:

What is the image of my deepest, innermost Self?

Allow yourself to continue asking this question as you work with one of these methods. The image will present itself, though it may take time and several sessions. Once you have it, you can come back to it anytime to ground yourself in strength and empowerment.

Chapter Resources

Learning your somatic yes and no

Your body generates different energies when your intuition says **yes** *versus when it says* **no**.

Sit quietly and softly speak the word *no* aloud—you will be able to feel the word in your body. Images of *no* in different forms may arise. Become acquainted with how this feels in every part of your body. Breathe deeply for several minutes and learn what *no* feels like.

Then, sit quietly and softly speak the word *yes*. Allow any images to arise as you breathe deeply and continue to say *yes*. Feel the difference in your body and take note of the experience of *yes*.

It may take time to learn how these words feel in your system, especially if your intuition has been blocked for any reason throughout your life.

Learning to hear the depths of your intuition means knowing when your inner guidance is saying *yes* and when it is saying *no*. The challenge will be acting from this deeper knowing.

Sound

In my last days in the big, bright ICU room, the pandemic lockdowns hit. I freaked out. The cancer was in my lungs—surely if I got COVID I would be a goner. My Brightest Self spent the rest of my hospital stay researching gas masks and purchasing bulk peanut butter on the internet. I received more chemotherapy and was sent home—mostly intact, but in a state of uncertainty about the future for us all.

I had only been home for a day or two when I took another nosedive. I awoke hardly able to keep my head up. I couldn't concentrate, and it felt challenging to make words. We checked my blood pressure and it was incredibly low. My whole body was pounding. I tried to get some iron and other minerals into my system with food and drink, but it did not help. A call to the doctor and we were back on the road to the cancer center, again. I felt wretched and smashed down, again. Scared and distraught, again.

Was this going to be my life for months? In and out of the hospital? Thinking I was feeling better, only to be squashed to pieces by my own body? I was so dismayed.

❧

A few months prior, a special book had landed in my life. *The Healing Power of Sound: Recovery from Life-Threatening Illness Using Sound,*

Voice, and Music was an enthralling read. It was written by the late Dr. Mitchell Gaynor, an oncologist who used sound healing techniques successfully as complementary treatment with his cancer patients. It is a fascinating exploration of how sound can be used to support healing even in the midst of toxic medical interventions. Through the use of singing bowls, breathing practices, chanting, toning, and classical music—all combined with guided meditation—Dr. Gaynor tells the stories of humans breaking through illness to find balance and harmony. The resonance I feel with his work continues to impact me; sound healing is central to my journey and my current professional life.

This book helped me understand how I could transform the energy in a room with a singing bowl or other instrument. Using sound alone or with others, I could find peace in my body in a way that other modalities didn't provide. Dr. Gaynor documents the amazing healing value of music and emphasizes how frequencies affect the energy bodies—while still acknowledging the good of Western medicine. Sometimes a person needs chemotherapy, and it will save their life. Western medicine is particularly great for acute situations, but weaving in complementary methods to create an integrative approach offers a wider potential for healing.

At the time of my diagnosis, I had become particularly interested in the frequency of 432 Hz. The internet seemed to love this frequency for its calming effect, and I had recently begun listening to a simple audio recording of it mixed with the sound of rain. These days I am uncertain whether there is anything particularly special about 432—I believe it is one of many healing frequencies that we can use to shift patterns and release blockages in the body, mind, and spirit—but you never know, maybe it is special.

On the road back to the hospital, my head hanging, I listened to this frequency and the rain through my headphones. It was the only way I could keep from falling to pieces. The feeling of utter helplessness—complete confusion about what was happening in my body—eased. I kept the audio in for hours as I was moved around in a wheelchair, put through tests, finally hooked onto an IV that proved helpful, and admitted to the hospital yet again.

I felt awful. And what felt even more awful was the idea that I would be feeling awful like this for the next four months or so. I was only a couple of weeks into this treatment, and I could not fathom continuing like this for long. *How was I going to survive this chemotherapy until June?*

I was still in the induction phase, which included the drug cisplatin. Cisplatin and other platinum-based chemotherapies are older drugs that are still widely used. They can be harsher than some of the newer treatments. Side effects of cisplatin include hearing loss, neuropathy, and blood deficiencies.

Back in a hospital room. *Beep, beep, beep.* Someone dug into my arm again to hook up an IV—to no avail. I couldn't take it anymore.

Dr. Davidson entered the room: *click, click, click.* She was looking fresh and beautiful as she came over to the side of my bed and stooped down to meet my eye level.

"This...is terrible." I told her.

"I know." She said, with true empathy. "But I really think it is going to get better when you no longer have to receive cisplatin. You were supposed to do one more induction infusion, but I am going to go ahead and move you to the standard treatment."

I hoped she was right. Stuffed inside that little hospital room with the cement block walls again, I felt so small, helpless and constrained. I just wanted to feel the movement of my body, to breathe, to feel light, and to live my life without fear.

I looked at her, exasperated. Then I looked at my arms, and sighed as tears welled up: "I need a port."

She nodded vigorously.

"Yes. Let's get you a port as soon as possible. I will go order it now." And she clicked out of the room.

I put my headphones back on and let the rain and the frequency wash over me. There was liberation in these sounds, and I could feel them creep in, releasing anxiety and leading me to just a touch of peace on this treacherous path.

⚬◇⚬

A few hours later they wheeled me off for the port installation. I lay in a surgical room under partial anesthesia as they put the robot box in my chest and a tube up the side of my neck. At least there wouldn't be any more digging.

The port was on the right side, sitting below my collar bone on my ribcage. It moved every time I took a breath, drawing my attention to my lungs and my chest—to the place where there were so many tumors. The tube from the port slithered up my neck like a visible worm underneath my skin. How odd it was to have such a contraption in my body; how inhuman it made me feel. Tagged as a patient; as one who needed help and care, as one who was struggling and was weak. Perhaps as one who was pitied. I did not care for any of this.

⚬◇⚬

Back in the hospital room again, I returned to my headphones, to sound—to solace.

⚬◇⚬

Throughout my treatment, my recovery, and into my current life's work, the superpower of sound amazes me and brings me deep peace. Sound is the space where math meets spirituality—where my two academic degrees start to make sense together. During my recovery from chemotherapy, I dug into the methods of toning and using tuning forks both on the body and in the field around the body. I experienced the power of singing alone and with others. I learned more about the influence of spoken words and tone to shift our states of consciousness. I am regularly astonished by the effects of sound on the entire human system.

The world is sound: all that exists is made up of frequency, of vibration all the way to a cellular level. We are patterns and we can repattern toward harmony through *entrainment*. The idea of entrainment is fundamental to all work with sound—objects and people will shift their vibrations to be in resonance with their surroundings. Therefore, we can introduce specific frequencies to make shifts in the body. Entrainment is natural and its effects become stronger with time.

Sound healing might include the use of the human voice in guided meditation, speaking stories, toning, singing and chanting. The complex frequencies of the voice can induce healing within the self or another. External sound healing sources such as recorded binaural beats, singing bowls, tuning forks or other instruments are also incredibly impactful. Binaural beats use two different frequencies—one in each ear—to specifically shift the brainwave state. Tuning forks and singing bowls will usually create an alpha or theta state, and their frequencies impact the energetic systems more directly in the whole body and field. In my recovery years I would learn about the uniquely healing effects of harmonic intervals.

All of these methods are remarkable resources during the whole experience of chemotherapy. These tools are not just soothing; they enhance and facilitate the entire healing process by repatterning energy and creating subtle but powerful shifts in the body, mind and spirit. There are so many empowering ways for you to use sound on your journey through chemotherapy and beyond.

Sound

Toning [7]

This is a simple method developed by Laurel Elizabeth Keyes. The idea is that you express the sounds that need to be expressed from your body to release tension, repattern, and shift toward wholeness.

Begin by standing with your feet hip-width apart. Bring your arms out to a T-position, with your shoulders dropped and loose. Close your eyes.

Begin to sway in a way that is comfortable for you and experience the natural pulsating rhythm of life.

Bring your awareness to your feet, and allow this awareness to travel up your legs, into your torso, and through your chest to your throat area.

Relax your jaw, and when it feels natural, allow sound to come out. Begin with low groans if you can. Groaning will release physical and emotional pain in your subconscious.

Building on the groan, allow your body to release any sounds that are needed. Continue swaying and feeling into the energy of life all around and within. The sound will likely rise and dip at different points. This should be experienced as effortless and without thought.

This session can last as long as you need. You will know when it is over because you will feel yourself involuntarily sigh and you will experience a sense of satisfaction and closure.

Chapter Resources

Chanting[8]

Chanting lies somewhere between talking and singing and usually uses simple sounds repetitively to elicit a rhythmic experience in the body. Chanting can take so many different forms—from chanting one syllable or word to basic phrases. Dr. Gaynor gave this method of chanting HU (pronounced "hue", the basic sound that connects us to our heart center) to connect with the self and the Divine.

Breathe in and out through the nose for one minute, thinking but not speaking the sound HU.

Breathe in and out through the mouth for one minute, chanting HU on the exhale.

Breathe in through your mouth and out through your nose for one minute, thinking but not speaking the sound HU.

Breathe in through your nose and out through your mouth for one minute, chanting HU on each exhale.

Sound With a Singing Bowl or Tuning Fork

You will need a singing bowl or 1-2 tuning forks. There are so many different notes and frequencies for these instruments that you can purchase. My suggestions for first forks are 256 Hz (C) and 384 Hz (G), which creates the perfect fifth harmonic. A 128 Hz fork with a crystal gem foot is also a favorite for use directly on the body. For a singing bowl, I suggest an F or C note.

Chapter Resources

The practice is simple:

Find a comfortable seat and play the bowl or fork. If you have forks, they can be used on the body or held up to the head. Feel yourself come into resonance and hum or sing along with the sound. Do this for as long as you wish.

Binaural Beats

The brain naturally moves through five different states of consciousness that coincide with brainwave frequencies:

Gamma, 35+ Hz. The state of consciousness in which we process information, learn, concentrate, and solve problems.

Beta, 12-35 Hz. The state of consciousness in which we are alert and attentive with a more relaxed focus.

Alpha, 8-12 Hz. The state of consciousness in which we are relaxed and our attention is more passive.

Theta, 4-8 Hz. The state of consciousness in which we are very deeply relaxed and inwardly focused.

Delta, 0.5-4 Hz. Deep sleep.

The brainwave states are created through the difference between the frequencies that are used in each ear (for example, 256 Hz in one ear and 266 Hz in the other ear creates a difference of 10 Hz, which is theta state).

I often used theta during chemotherapy to ensure a deep state of relaxation, and delta if I was struggling with insomnia. You can find audio recordings of binaural beats on YouTube or music streaming platforms.

Nourishment

Dr. Davidson was right; the cisplatin had been rough on me. When I began the standard treatment, my body settled down. For the next couple of months, I found a rhythm in this new life as a cancer patient.

Every Thursday I had chemotherapy. The pandemic had shut the world down, so I was no longer allowed any visitors. I went in for my treatment alone, every week, for a long time. Chemotherapy alternated week-by-week: inpatient, outpatient, inpatient, outpatient. I would get dropped off at the front of the hospital or the cancer center and make my way inside—mask on, hat or head scarf on my head. Comfy, warm clothes because I knew the chemo would make me cold. I had a rainbow flower backpack filled with books and supplies.

I spent the time journaling, listening to meditations and sounds, chatting with nurses, and reading—generally trying to distract myself from the poison entering my body. *Drip, drip, drip.* The hospital became familiar. *Beep, beep beep.* It wasn't the life I wanted, but I made it work.

My hCG steadily decreased with each round of chemotherapy; my blood tests showed that I was headed in the right direction. But it felt so slow, and the number was never as low as I hoped it would be. I chugged along, trying to live my life as usual—as if that were even possible. I didn't have a job to keep my mind occupied, so I spent my time reading more about healing, doing my self-care practices, playing with Elsie and Beatrice as much as I could, and trying to just stay afloat. I dreamed of turning our land into a working farm and gathering space, so I put effort into website building during this time—but it would become another of my ideas that would never see the finish line.

⸎

The middle of May arrived. My hCG came in at 317, which meant I still had many rounds of chemo ahead of me. I would not be finished with treatment by June, and these unmet expectations began to feel heavy. *How long was this going to last? Surely, I would be done by early August?* That felt far, far away.

The weight of powerlessness began to take its toll. The light was becoming lackluster.

I wanted to feel a semblance of control over this situation—to do *something* that might help. Maybe if I tightened up my diet again all of this would heal.

⸎

Food has been complicated for me since I was ten years old. I have struggled to find the balance between eating too much and not eating enough—and experienced seasons of both uncontrollable eating and tightly controlled eating. Either way, these issues were tied together in my history: food had to do with control. Food was stressful. Sometimes it still is.

⸎

I thought I was well-versed in the different ways a cancer patient might find nutritional support. There are so many ideas floating around: some experts advocate for a vegan diet, while others claim keto works best. Some say the ancestral diet will provide the most nutrients, others say we should live on green juice. What are we supposed to do in this age of abundant, conflicting information?

Throughout my treatment, I trusted the research of the Block Center. *Life Over Cancer: The Block Center Program for Integrative Cancer Treatment* written by Keith Block, MD was a go-to for integrative practices and protocols. They fall into the vegan camp and are adamantly against animal products if you have cancer, with well-backed experience and research.

After my first blood transfusions early in treatment, I scoured the internet for the most effective sources of iron. I found beef spleen, and began taking a supplement in capsule form. It didn't fit into the Block Center's plan, but it seemed to be what my body needed at the time. I felt more energetic soon after beginning my beef spleen regimen—it was a small choice I made that I believe was greatly beneficial for me during that time.

In the early weeks of treatment, I was pretty strict: no sugar, meat, dairy, or gluten—with the exception of the beef spleen. I drank a lot of green juice. It was the low-sugar kind, fresh from the juicer, expensive and time-consuming (thank you to Matt, who spent the time chopping and juicing). It felt good in my body, but it grew tiring for everyone, and gradually it left my nutritional rotation. I found an organic green powdered supplement to be an adequate stand-in.

The conflicting information about food made my head spin, and I wanted to trust my intuition, but I wasn't always sure my body was able to communicate with me properly with all the toxins floating about. I kept working on my ability to listen inwardly and make healthy choices.

With June approaching, I wanted some additional ideas and support—perhaps I could speed up this process a little bit by controlling my food in a different way. After a thorough internet search, I consulted Dr. Dave Allderdice, a naturopathic physician who specializes in integrative cancer care at the Sage Cancer Center in Portland, Oregon. We met via Zoom—he was sincere, knowledgeable, and relaxed. I needed this. Dr. Dave pointed me to a balanced nutritional approach during chemotherapy which proved greatly helpful: eat whole foods most of the time, listen to the wisdom of your body, fill it with nutrients, add some supportive supplements (he suggested, for me, medicinal mushrooms, curcumin, magnolia bark, and melatonin). Dr. Dave also made the mind-blowing suggestion that I not stress out too much about food. While on chemotherapy, he said it's really the chemotherapy that is doing the work, so don't eat McDonald's every day, but also—eat some ice cream sometimes, and enjoy it. *Stress is not nutritional.*

I made a variation of the veggie broth Dr. Dave suggested and sipped on it during and between treatments. I loved the green and red powdered supplements I found, and stuck with Dr. Dave's recommended supplements, too. I stayed as hydrated as I could to move the chemotherapy through my body. Some days after chemo I didn't feel like eating anything but eggs. Sometimes I wanted some pizza. I tried to eat whole foods incorporating a variety of colors, to not go overboard on anything, and to limit the foods that didn't feel good in my body.

The earth holds so much of what we need to nourish ourselves. The more we eat from the earth, the healthier we will feel. But life does not always allow a farm-to-table existence, so balance is crucial. Focusing on the positive was a helpful practice for me: I tried to make sure to fill myself with nourishing whole foods from the earth as much as I could. Sometimes there were treat foods, and I decided not to feel guilty or tense about them.

Turning focus from what *not to eat* (gluten, dairy, sugar, corn, soy, meat, etc.) to what *to eat* (plenty of vibrantly-colored whole foods) was profound for me: *positive nourishment*. Stress is not nutritional. My long history of tension around food began to transform during my treatment—it is still in process, but I have come a long way. I am trying to let go, rather than control. To nourish myself in ways that relieve stress rather than create it.

Finding a way to eat that works for you might be a deeper journey than you expect. Focus on whole foods as much as you can, and listen to your body. Consider your historic relationship with food and how it is affecting your experience, and if you are interested in more specific supplement support, I recommend consulting with a professional. A naturopathic or integrative physician or nutritionist who specializes in oncology can tailor recommendations to your unique cancer and treatment.

Nourishment

Veggie Broth Recipe

Sip this broth anytime or use it as the base for other nutritional soups that you enjoy.

Ingredients:

2 large onions

2 heads of garlic

6 large carrots

1 bunch of celery

2 sweet potatoes

2-3 cups of any type of mushroom

1 strip of kombu or other seaweed

1 bunch of parsley

¼ c. of apple cider vinegar

Fresh rosemary

Fresh thyme

Black peppercorns

Salt to taste

Instructions:

Rinse all of the ingredients and chop them into chunks. The size isn't important, just make sure they will fit into the pot and that they have been opened up via at least one slicing.

Put everything except the salt into a 12-quart or larger stockpot and fill it with filtered water. Water should cover the vegetables by at least a couple of inches.

Bring everything to a boil and then cover and simmer for at least four hours. You may need to add more water to make up for evaporation along the way.

Strain the broth and then add the salt. Let it cool thoroughly before storing. This will last about five days in the refrigerator or several months in the freezer.

Useful Additions and Supplements

- Powdered, organic greens
- Powdered, organic red fruits and vegetables
- Electrolyte powder or liquid for deep hydration
- Medicinal mushrooms (chaga, reishi, and turkey tail in particular) in capsule or powdered form
- Curcumin

Webs

The end of May arrived. I went in for my inpatient chemo—first to the cancer center for labs, then dropped off on the other side of campus at the hospital for my stay. I found my way into a hospital room on the ninth floor and settled in with some reading.

Lab results always come through via an email with a subject line that reads NEW TEST RESULTS—screaming at me in capital letters. Sometimes I would see the results before the doctors saw them; other times they would call me with the results before I had them. I saw the email first on this particular Thursday.

Given the current trajectory of my hCG level, I figured it would be somewhere around 100. I hoped for under 100. I took a deep breath and opened the email.

334. The number had gone up from the 317 of two weeks prior.

I felt crushed. I knew that feeling *crushed* was kind of unreasonable, since the increase wasn't that much, but that was how I felt. It felt like I would never be done with this chemotherapy. *June was going to happen in a couple of days—June! I was supposed to be done in June!*

I just sat there in the hospital bed, crying alone. Everything felt horrible. I was puffy and bloated and my hair looked weird and I just wanted to hang out with my children, actually. *Can I just feel better and be well and hang out with my children? Please?! And can whatever is beeping in this room stop, also??*

I was in the middle of an internal rant, probably speaking most of it aloud, actually, when the room phone rang. It was the first time that I remember this happening. *Am I supposed to pick it up?*

"...hello?"

"Hi Hannah, it's Dr. Watson." Dr. Watson was the new gynecological oncology fellow; Dr. Puechl had finished her term. She was calling to check in on me—she saw my labs and assumed I might be upset about them. She was reassuring, but I was still crying. She told me she would come down and see me soon. I sat and waited, alone and disappointed and sad.

Dr. Watson arrived in the room a few minutes later. She was tall, I think. She had brown hair and excellent bone structure. It must be some sort of rule that the beautiful doctors become gynecological oncologists.

She heard my disappointment, and she didn't gloss over the reality. This was all hard, and my case is particularly bad. This might not be straightforward. She was not sure who told me I would be done with treatment in June, but that wasn't a reasonable expectation. (I won't rat anyone out here, either!)

All I could do was keep going—receive more chemotherapy, *drip, drip, drip.* And wait for the next NEW TEST RESULTS.

Again my mind wandered to what I could possibly do to shift this situation—I am a problem solver, sometimes to a fault. I decided that what I needed now was to talk with someone who was going through the same thing. My type of cancer was rare, but I knew there were people out there dealing with this, too. Because of the quarantine, much of the support that would have usually been possible for a cancer patient was not available. My web of connection was limited to my family and the internet. The internet was marked by a collective energy of health fear during this pandemic time, so navigating all of the information was exceptionally challenging for me.

As I sat in the hospital that day, chemo dripping and spirit aching, I began an internet search for support. I joined a Facebook group and googled *Gestational Trophoblastic Neoplasia* and *choriocarcinoma*. I had mostly been avoiding using the web in this way up until this point, but I needed it now. What I found was that people mostly lived through this—just like my doctors told me—though the fact that it only affects mothers of newborns and very young children brings specific hardships. The Facebook group was helpful enough—it was filled with curiosities about chemotherapy symptoms and parenting tips for getting through this with little ones.

After soaking in the Facebook group for too long, I did some more searching and a new something popped up: *Esli's Choriocarcinoma Journey.* I clicked on the link—certainly, this person was going through the same nightmare that I was. She had three little girls and lived in South Africa. I sent her a message, and we became internet friends.

I know that internet friends are not the same as in-person friends. I have learned that the connections we create on social media are inferior to those we create with humans whose voices and facial expressions and hugs we get to experience firsthand. Yet I also know there is a real way to connect with people from a distance—that distance and time are not always what they seem.

Esli was diagnosed just a couple of weeks after I was. With an hCG level very high like mine, she too was *high-risk*. She had been interested in an alternative route of treatment and so began her chemotherapeutic journey with a lighter load of poison paired with IVs of holistic immune system boosters. I could tell from photos and from these messages how beautiful she was in her whole being. We wrote to one another about what was helping us, what we were afraid of, what was joyful, and what was challenging. A friend for the journey was an indispensable resource.

⚬⚭⚬

Trees are social beings. Tree friends share nutrients through their roots; they practice interdependence by connecting to one another through these systems in the soil. They are especially prone to sharing in times of need. Trees, on their own, cannot establish a consistent local climate, but together they can create an ecosystem that is sustaining for the whole. The trees communicate via electricity—sound waves, actually. Trees nourish one another through their roots and through the energy of sound.

⚬⚭⚬

The importance of having a tree friend cannot be overstated. Esli was on the other side of the world, yet she brought me comfort and support in a way that no one else could. Our friendship had roots in the experience of this cancer, and we were able to offer nourishment to one another in various forms. The people in close physical proximity to me did everything they could; they took care of my children and cooked and gave me hugs when I was down. They held hope for me when I was not able to hold it for myself. I have deep gratitude for the support I received from my family and friends. But having a friend who was going through the same thing was vital, too.

Esli believed in the healing power of the Holy Spirit. As it turns out, I believe in it, too. But healing takes on different forms and is not always what we picture. Time is different than I thought before all of this happened—it is more mysterious than it is clear and straightforward. Healing is not always about physical health in this lifetime—healing is a soul experience. This is what I learned from Esli: to be confident in healing from God in the midst of a complex experience, to listen deeply to the whispers of the Spirit even when they don't make sense, to care for the body with every fiber of your being.

Later in my journey, I would find another friend, this time a person who had finished treatment and gone through quite the rough experience. Ferris had been through several lines of chemotherapy before she landed on an immunotherapy that was successful for her. She had been in and out of treatment for three years, and her story both frightened me and gave me hope. I very much did not want to go through many lines of treatment. But eventually, Ferris made it through, and that was an encouraging story for me to hear. Ferris became another friend whose prayers and cheerleading were crucial for my recovery.

I found both of my cancer friends on the internet—I know that the internet is not all bad. It offers us access to incredibly useful information and connects us with people in ways that would otherwise be impossible. I am grateful for the cancer friends I found this way.

But I had to be careful and discerning about technology because the wider community was a different story. Input from the global consciousness was intense during COVID-19: the fear of death was palpable, and the web was buzzing with anxiety. Limiting my internet exposure was one way of creating a necessary boundary for myself to heal. This meant that sometimes I was uninformed about the state of the world, but that was the only way I could maintain my sanity.

Navigating the loads of information we receive from the internet is challenging for everyone. I don't believe humans are wired to know everything that is going on all over the world all of the time—it is simply too much heartbreak for any person to hold. We are wired for deep connections with our local community and land, to be able to handle the hardships that come in those spaces. Yet, the internet is an amazing tool for learning and resourcing one another.

It is even more challenging to navigate these issues when going through a medical crisis. On one hand, sometimes we stumble upon information or online groups that are encouraging and hopeful. On the other hand, the internet will always scare the crap out of us. In most cases, if you google a health issue, it will tell you that you are dying, or that you will be dying in the very near future, even if you don't have cancer. If you do have cancer, it will be very easy to find fatal cases no matter your prognosis. It was not useful for me to look up and ruminate over the statistics of my particular situation. Anytime I did this I sent myself into a spiral of stress. I suggest avoiding this kind of web searching if you can—statistics are just numbers, and they do not account for the whole story. Your story is yours, and it may or may not go the same way as the majority of people with your cancer. Even with my rare and particular cancer, the two friends I made had different stories and outcomes than I did.

You may need to give yourself permission to create a healthy boundary with the global community, with the swirling information all around. Tending to yourself is not selfish. Respect yourself enough to know when enough is enough and draw boundaries when needed.

It took a lot of trial and error for me to find balance with the interweb. I ended up taking a long break from social media during this year to focus on my local experience. You will have to tune in to figure out the balance for yourself. Check in regularly about whether the information you are absorbing is helpful or harmful. Don't be afraid to say *no* to the abundance of swirling news, stories, and videos if that would support your well-being. Creating a healthy web for myself by finding tree friends with whom I shared roots and being conscious and discerning about the technology was crucial throughout my treatment.

Webs

Find a friend

Find a friend or two who are going through the same cancer. Check local support groups, ask your doctor, or use the World Wide Web responsibly.

Limit the Internet

Use the internet when it will be helpful and life-giving; try not to google your diagnosis too much. Remember that statistics are just numbers, and they don't represent the whole story.

Establish Healthy Boundaries

You may need to create clear boundaries for yourself. Say *no* when you need to say *no*, spend time with people who make you feel empowered and bright, and give yourself permission to not absorb all of the information and news.

Put Yourself in a Pineapple[9]

That's right, a pineapple. I learned this exercise in my recovery years from my creative speech teacher at Waldorf teacher training. It uses sound and visualization to create a firm but kind energetic boundary around you while helping you to maintain a bright core self (just like a pineapple).

Chapter Resources

Stand up and find firm grounding in your feet. Hold your hands in light fists, thumb and pointer finger together in such a way that you can *fist-point*.

Imagine yourself the bright and juicy inside of a pineapple.

Make the sound "dih" repeatedly as you use your fist-points to mark the outer edge of the pineapple. You are creating a boundary that is strong but not harmful to anyone else.

Do this until you feel adequately bright and juicy—yet also contained and safe from any overwhelming external sources.

Mistletoe

Rewind to the first days after diagnosis. I was in the whirlwind of tests and new poisons in my body. My sister, Claire, was in the hospital room with me. Claire is six years younger than me, naturally blond with aquamarine eyes. She was a Waldorf teacher at the time, and had moved to the area the year before to work at the school in Chapel Hill. This was the first time we have lived in the same city in a decade. Our relationship had waxed and waned over the years—we're siblings, after all. We are quite different humans; and we have a good many commonalities. She used to steal my clothes, and I can be annoyingly bossy. Secretly, I think she's amazing. Her life has been winding, too, but she doesn't seem to be having panic attacks. She must be stronger than me, but big sisters don't always remember to tell little sisters such things.

Claire lightly suggested that I look into some mistletoe treatment, a remedy from her Waldorf circles. I think I thanked her for the suggestion—but I don't know. I was still in shock that first week, and filed the mistletoe away for another day.

⌒∞⌒

Waldorf Education was founded by a man named Rudolf Steiner in the early 20th century. There is beauty in the educational pedagogy: students experience much time in nature, don't use screens in class until high school, and visual art and storytelling are deeply woven into the curriculum. There is a spiritual understanding of the human and the way that development unfolds.

Steiner wrote and lectured profusely on matters of education, esoteric spirituality, healing and medicine, farming, and social reform, which all gave rise to a movement called *anthroposophy*. The internet says that anthroposophy is a "spiritual new religious movement," and at its worst, it has been labeled a cult. But anthroposophy means "wisdom of the human being," and in my experience, it seeks to bring our innate spiritual wisdom and perception into our everyday lives.

One of the branches of anthroposophy is anthroposophic medicine. Mistletoe is an anthroposophical remedy used to fight cancer, sometimes alone and sometimes as a complementary treatment. Mistletoe therapy uses a European species of the plant for the treatment of cancer, widely offered in Europe as a complementary treatment, and currently undergoing U.S. clinical trials at Johns Hopkins University. Treatment with mistletoe can be provided in a stronger form via IV at select medical centers or administered by injection at home.

June arrived. I had planned for it to be over by now, to be moving on with my life. I had a vision for a farm space I called Solace Hill—a healing place for people to gather and grow together. But that wouldn't happen, either—the world was in quarantine, and I had no energy for it. My cancer was still active in my body. I was emotionally and spiritually exhausted. The hope and energy that I had felt early in my treatment were waning, and I began to feel desperate, like I would never get out of this. I was a prisoner to the poison, to the cancer and chemotherapy in my body, to the fear and loneliness in my spirit. They were all relentless.

I dug out the mistletoe from the back of my mind and decided that it was time to track some down. Claire had been busy that spring with quarantine/Zoom teaching and she often cared for my girls in any free time she had. I went back to her with the subject of mistletoe and she connected me with a person in the Waldorf community who connected me with an anthroposophical doctor who wrote me a prescription. It was relatively simple: I would inject myself (or have someone else inject me) three times a week with a solution that needed to be prescribed and ordered from a special pharmacy. This doctor had seen wonderful results, decreasing the side effects of chemotherapy significantly. I asked her if I could just go off chemotherapy and do this instead. She told me that, no, this would not cure my cancer, but it would increase my quality of life while going through treatment and likely be useful for a time after treatment in preventing recurrence.

Mistletoe—the one we hang in doorways at Christmastime to catch people and force them to smooch? I was already accustomed to using plants and herbs for healing, but I was not familiar with this one.

I did some research. Mistletoe is a hemiparasite, which means that it is parasitic—it grows on other plants and takes their nutrients for its own survival—but it also conducts photosynthesis, so in theory it could live on its own. Sometimes mistletoe even kills trees by stealing so many of their nutrients that they are no longer able to live.

There are myths about mistletoe that go back thousands of years. In Ancient Greece it was a symbol of male fertility, the Celtic Druids used it in their rituals, the Romans saw it as a representation of peace and understanding. Norse legends began the custom of passing beneath the mistletoe in a gesture of love. One Norse myth says that if two enemies landed underneath the mistletoe together they had to lay down their weapons and call a truce.

Eventually the myth shifted and was embraced by the English in the 1800s, and we have been using it for kissing ever since. It is this same species of mistletoe *(viscum album)* that has been used for anticancer treatment since the 1920s.

Mistletoe is complex, strong, and exceptionally healing.

I began the injections and immediately felt a difference in my energy level. The mistletoe gave me a lightness that helped me move about with more ease. I felt stronger, and that was worth something. It was relatively cost-efficient, and Dr. Davidson didn't have a problem with me using it. I was always careful to inform her of what I was doing, as some complementary therapies can react with chemotherapy. I continued mistletoe injections every three days for the remainder of my cancer treatment, and for a year after. I definitely recommend mistletoe and wish I had started it sooner. A big thank you to Claire for pointing me to mistletoe—complex, strong, and exceptionally healing.

Mistletoe

Find an Anthroposophical Doctor

This website lists anthroposophical medicine providers, many of whom can prescribe mistletoe from a distance.

https://anthroposophicmedicine.org/provider-directory

Believe Big Foundation

This organization supports cancer patients and mistletoe research and provides valuable resources:

https://www.believebig.org

Interlude

I needed a pause button. I just wanted to be a regular human being, if only for a few moments. Sickness had become my identity—it was hard to differentiate the true self from the cancer self.

I was so tired of being Cancer Patient. My head scarf and my robot chest box were such a part of me at this point that I began to forget I had ever been anyone else.

One day, I remembered: *I think I used to like laughter. Did life used to be funny? Was laughing with other humans once my favorite thing?*

I ordered a new notebook. I have an indescribable love for new notebooks. This one was red with a hardcover, of the Moleskine variety.

I wrote in the front of the book: *What's funny?* And I decided that I would document the most hilarious parts of this journey. Anytime I saw something funny, I would take note. Surely there was an unseen world of comedy just waiting to be found at the Duke Cancer Center and on the ninth floor of the hospital.

What's Funny? has only one entry:

> *July 9, 2020*
> > *Bald people continue to be funny.*
> > *Got cancer? Under 40? Stupid Cancer®*
> > *(good-looking bald guy clearly does not have cancer)*

Here is what I remember: I sat in the waiting room at the cancer center with my red notebook. I looked up and saw that there were...*bald* people everywhere. Like I saw it. I zoomed out and realized where I was. I had been around bald people for months but never had I realized how odd it was to be sitting in a large room filled with almost exclusively bald people. We were quarantined, so no one was allowed visitors. It was just us Cancer Patients. And most of us were bald or bald-ish. Just a bunch of bald people with robot chest boxes. Like being on another planet.

Later that day, I walked through the ninth-floor halls of the hospital toward my room, and I stumbled upon a poster on the wall. It had a young, good-looking guy on it with full, bushy eyebrows. He looked pretty healthy—but he was bald. Now, a bald cancer patient would certainly not have eyebrows this bushy.

The poster, by an organization called Stupid Cancer®, reads, *Got cancer?* in the style of a *Got milk?* ad. Like cancer and milk are somehow on the same level, in the same category? I floated off into my imagination, where two good-looking dudes, healthy but bald, with nice bushy eyebrows, run into one another:

Dude #1 *[holding a glass of milk]*: "Oh hey! How's it goin'? I got some milk. I'm just here drinking it. It's delicious. What's up with you, dude...what do you got?"
Dude #2: "Oh hey. Yeah, I got something, too....it's...cancer. I got...cancer."

Awkward silence.

D1: "Whoa. Um...well....that's...........................stupid."

More awkward silence.

D2: "Dude. You're right...it *is* stupid. I never really thought about how stupid it is before. Stupid...cancer. It's like the most stupid of all the stupid stuff."
D1: "Totally. Stupid. Cancer."

More awkward silence.

D2: "Whoa dude. This is, like, blowing my mind. Stupid Cancer."
D1: "Stupid Cancer! I bet Stupid Cancer would blow a lot of people's minds."
D2: "Dude! Totally! It's like a totally mind-blowing idea!...We gotta trademark this, right now. Stupid Cancer ®"

You will need interludes on this stupid chemotherapeutic journey. I know that cancer is decidedly not funny. And yet, the therapeutic qualities of humor and laughter cannot be overstated. You know what's funny to you, so make that happen as much as possible.

(I know now that Stupid Cancer® is working to make adolescent and young adult cancer "suck less," so... I'm...sorry?)

Water

My father, Michael, is Catholic. I am not.
I grew up with two significant church experiences. One was a large, fancy Episcopal Church in the suburbs of Louisville, Kentucky. There were a lot of people, big windows, and a set liturgy that was simultaneously comforting and off-putting for me. We kneeled at the altar and took communion in the form of wafers and port wine. The place felt cold, yet over the years I would develop warm relationships with many of the people there.

The other church was Galilee Christian Church in Burtonville, Kentucky—near the farm where my grandparents lived. It was small, with carpeted pews and a preacher I don't remember. The Sunday school rooms in the basement had cement floors and walls. These spaces had a distinct smell that I can't describe.

I would ride with my Papaw in his white truck to church on Sunday mornings when I was visiting, and he'd wave with one finger to each car we passed. He always wore his light blue suit and a hat—the same suit he was buried in years later. He and A.A. sat in the same place every week in the little church room, filled mostly with elderly people and a few grandchildren running around. They sang old hymns with off-pitched voices and passed around tiny rectangular communion crackers with cups of grape juice. I don't remember what they said about God. But I remember the songs, the smells, and the feeling of being welcomed.

In my early years, I played priest in the living room at my home. I would speak the service from a stolen *Book of Common Prayer* to my two-person congregation of willing parents and serve communion in the form of Trident gum and cran-raspberry juice—a mash-up of my two different experiences of communion and ritual. Something about the gathering of people for spiritual practice has always drawn me in.

After college, I became interested in reading theology and found books about other strains of Christianity that fascinated me. I stumbled into Christian ideologies that promoted nonviolence, social justice, communities of hospitality and contemplative practice. These felt new and fresh to me.

I found myself in North Carolina at Duke Divinity School. I twisted and turned through various denominations, trying to fit myself into religious boxes that were never quite the right size or shape. My relationship with the church and with the Christian religion waxed and waned in the 15 years to come. I left the Episcopal Church and joined the United Church of Christ. I left it all, then went back. I have found myself in a pattern of leaving and re-entering these religious spaces, always uncertain of where or if I belong. Religious life and my spiritual experience seem disconnected: church has felt like a chore to complete in order to make others happy, but my experience of God is real. Eventually, my interest in the mystics and a more contemplative expression of spirituality would settle in. But there are thousands of forms of Christianity, all claiming they know what it means to be Christian—so vastly different that they could be viewed as separate religions. *Am I any of these?* Can I use the word *Christian* for myself knowing how troubling it is for people who have experienced harm in churches: exclusivity and hypocrisy, patriarchy and silencing? I grappled with the ways this religion has been a key player in colonialism and slavery and indigenous genocide. These are questions worth my struggle and contemplation.

Divinity school gave me a lot of time to think and overthink theology. I had no trouble experiencing God as Light or Infinite Love, but I often lost this experience in the details and structure of the church. The freedom to hold Mystery is crucial for my spiritual life.

These religious experiences and questions have played an important role in my life, whether I like it or not. The narratives shape my imagination; the churches are part of my identity.

⁂

During the months of first line treatment, I settled into a rhythm: chemo on Thursdays, feel my worst Friday through Sunday, and then feel pretty well and able to carry out the usual tasks from Monday through Wednesday. I put one foot in front of the other in a practical way, trying to make plans and schedules for the future. I was not particularly in touch with my feelings; I was just trying to make it through. I followed the guidelines, lived in the system, and managed as well as possible. But this rhythm grew tired, and July neared its end. I was nowhere near the finish line—my expectations of being finished with treatment had been smashed to bits. The pattern that I thought I could follow seemed to be breaking down, my spirit with it.

Dad arrived at the farmhouse to pick up the girls one day, and he handed me a gift: a Catholic first aid kit that included a rosary, a small metal icon of Mary and baby Jesus, and a bottle of blessed water from Lourdes. He didn't say much, but gave me a crinkled smile with his baby blue eyes. He thought it might lift my spirits and explained a little bit about where the items had come from.

Dad had become Catholic a few years prior; religion has always been of utmost importance to him. I wasn't immediately sure what to do with the little gifts, not being Catholic and what not. I was grateful, though, and I put them in my satchel of special items that included Papaw's coin, some trinkets from my children, and a rose quartz crystal.

⚬⚭⚬

Many Catholics believe that the water from Lourdes has special healing properties. Tradition says that Mary appeared to Bernadette Soubirous in the mid-19th century, pointing her to the water at the Grotto of Massabielle. Since that time, many people have reported healings and miracles after drinking or bathing in this water.

Holy water had always seemed like a superstition to me: a symbol of something sacred, but not sacred itself.

No one had said much about Mary in the churches I had attended. Mother of Jesus, pregnant teenager—that's basically all I heard. Her stories were glossed over as were so many of the stories of women in the biblical narratives. *Who is this Mary?* I wondered as I held the little gifts given to me by my father. There was something about these items—the water in particular—that felt unusually sacred to me.

⚬⚭⚬

Around this time, I stumbled upon another book: *Cancer and the New Biology of Water* by Thomas Cowan, MD. This book looks to water as the source of life. "In order for there to be life, there must be water... where there is water, there will also be life." —it is a profoundly obvious statement. Dr. Cowan argues that it is the structure of water in cells that gives us health or unhealth. He believes that the deterioration of that water is the cause of cancer. Water brings a specific form to the atoms within the body, and a disruption of that form creates disease.[10]

146

Dr. Cowan has many suggestions for potential complementary cancer treatments in his book, but the one I integrated into my regimen was called Quinton isotonic water. This supplement was created by a person named René Quinton in the early 20th century and has been used successfully to support the healing of many challenging diseases over the years. Dr. Cowan recommends that any person who wants to maintain or improve their health take this supplement, as it is safe with demonstrated efficacy. Isotonic water provides essential trace minerals and has a composition that is similar to blood plasma. Folding it into my supplement routine gave me a sense of calm and additional hydration.

At some point I had started taking Epsom salt and baking soda baths. I learned from the internet that many people going through chemotherapy found these baths useful for moving the toxins through more quickly. This was the only time in my adult life that I enjoyed baths, and I found the warmth and water cleansing and comforting.

I drank as much water as I could to flush out the toxins, and the hydration was a saving grace. Adding some electrolytes helped. I spent time sitting on the ground by the pond on our land. Dr. Dave recommended cold water therapy to strengthen my immune system, so I attempted cold showers when I could stand them.

Water rushed into my life in many forms that summer.

A few weeks after receiving my Catholic gift, I took a soak, bagful of trinkets on the ledge of the tub. I found myself meditating in the bath quite frequently, often holding my coin or a crystal as I leaned into the silence and stillness. On this day, I floated into that space and the little Catholic objects seemed to find their way into my hands. I held the icon and absorbed the image of Mary holding a baby. Mary—the portal through which Jesus of Nazareth arrived into the world. The conduit of something that millions of people believe to be a miraculous, holy event. The whole narrative of Jesus's life, death, and resurrection was completely dependent on this first event of Mary giving birth. Many celebrate Christmas as the time Jesus came to earth—the coming of the light in darkness—but what of Mary? Was that moment not also about Mary's power to bring forth life?

I sat with the icon, and I sobbed. Something broke open in me—I had been holding back feelings, trying my best to make it through this experience, but there in the water I hit a limit. Mothering is enormously complex—relentless in what it asks of us on every level of our being. It is so much love to hold. What must it have felt like to Mother Mary? I held the icon for a long time, crying for myself and for all the mothers who struggled in all the ways that a mother might struggle—weeping with gratitude for the growing pains.

I cried, also, for my Grandmother Mary—the portal through which my father arrived in this world. I cried for the loneliness and the grief she must have experienced, for the challenges she faced in the medical system, too. For the tragedy of it all—*motherhood killed her*, I heard again. And I wondered, again, if motherhood would kill me too as I cried with Mother Mary and with Grandmother Mary. I opened the little bottle of holy water and poured its cool contents onto my head. Perhaps baptism comes in many forms.

I began to experience the story of Mary, Mother of Jesus, in a strong and healing way. There was something there for me, even if I struggled to name it. I could feel the traditions, the rituals, the sacred stories. I felt the holiness of the water in these moments; the Mystery of it cannot be understated.

These were my father's cosmic gestures of care: water to break me open and teach me fluidity, and sacred stories to hold me.

These are his holy gifts, given to me in different expressions since my childhood.

⁘

Water is the element of slow movement and flexibility, of depth and introspection. It is cleansing and revitalizing. It transforms from liquid to solid and creates intricate patterns. It holds memory. If the water element is stagnant, we hold our feelings in. If we allow it to heal us, we break the rigid patterns that keep us frozen.

I turned to water in many ways to bring harmony to my system during treatment.

Water

Drink Clean Water

Drink as much clean, filtered water as you can before, during, and after treatment. I recommend a Berkey or similar filter. Adding electrolytes or drinking broth are good alternatives if you are struggling to stomach unflavored water.

Salt and Soda Bath

Pour 1-2 cups of Epsom salts and 1 cup of baking soda into a warm bath and soak for at least 20 minutes. I recommend this soon after chemotherapy to get the medicine moving through more quickly. This combination has also been shown to have more subtle energetic cleansing effects.

Quinton Isotonic Water

1-3 doses per day of Quinton isotonic solution will help to rejuvenate and hydrate you at any point during your treatment.

Cold Water Therapy

At the end of a usual shower, turn the cold water on for 30-60 seconds (as long as you can stand it). This will stimulate your immune system. If you really like it, try an ice bath!

Holy Water

If there is a natural way for you to use water in a sacred manner, I suggest it as a cleansing ritual. This will depend on your own system and community, so I will not offer specifics.

Water Sounds

Audio recordings of rain and other water sounds can be soothing if you are struggling with rigidity or with accessing your feelings. Try turning these sounds on in your treatment room while receiving chemotherapy.

Water Imagery

Sit or lie down and settle in. Take several deep breaths.

Imagine yourself on the shore—the edge where the sand and the sea meet. Sink into the ground and experience all of the sensations that are present.

> *What do you smell? Taste? Feel with your skin? See with your eyes? Hear? What is more subtle all around you?*

Take another deep breath and experience the tide coming near. The water gently touches you with slow and kind movement, and any fear you are holding becomes part of the water. The wave recedes, back to the sea, taking your fear with it. Breathe slowly with the waves.

Allow yourself to stay here for as long as you would like, experiencing the cleansing action of the waves covering your body and then taking your fear back to the ocean. Fall into the rhythm of the waves, experiencing new fluidity, depth, and comfort with each movement of the water.

Collaboration

August in North Carolina is always hot and sticky. I had prickly bits of hair growing all over my head. My eyebrows were thinning. I had gained weight from the steroids. My skin had odd tints of yellow and gray. I didn't recognize myself in the mirror. I had received ten rounds of chemotherapy in addition to the two induction doses—well past the six to eight rounds that I had expected. My hCG level had plateaued around 50, and I was just trudging along.

The plateau had to continue for three rounds of treatment in a row for me to be declared *chemo-resistant* to this concoction and moved to the next line of treatment. We had come a long way in terms of the amount of cancer—there was actually very little left in my body. But we needed to get all of it because of how aggressively this kind of cancer grows.

Emotional and spiritual exhaustion had seeped in slowly. I didn't look like myself, but I had more energy than expected at this point. The resources I was integrating into my routine were definitely helping my physical self, but the deeper parts of me were weakening.

The idea of *chemo-resistance* was new to me. I always thought a person could just receive as much chemotherapy as needed until their body could no longer handle the poison. This is not the case. Bodies start to assimilate and eventually the drugs stop working. The task is to stay healthy enough to receive the treatment and also support the chemotherapy toward efficacy.

What would happen if I became resistant to this treatment? Would I move to a second and become resistant to that, too? Was I going to go through this whole chemo process uncured? How long would I last after that? These were the questions that cycled in my mind all the humid summer long. All I could do was wait to see my hCG number every two weeks. Wait and be patient. Try to live life in the usual manner. Except we were living in a pandemic, and there was cancer, and nothing was in the usual manner.

I was impatient. Impatient and confused, because I was doing everything I knew how to do, yet the cancer still lingered. I was beginning to have a hard time getting myself to take walks or do any sort of exercise. I felt defeated—low and slow. Patience is already a tough practice for me, as it is for many of us. We live in a culture of immediate gratification: we can instantly access information, shop for anything we want to buy, binge watch as many episodes as we want. It seemed like I should be able to snap my fingers and just *heal already*.

So I attempted patience, until I got the official news that I had become chemo-resistant to the EMA-CO. The extent of my disease was too much for the first line of chemotherapy to finish off. I was ultra high-risk, after all—my doctors did well to remind me of this. But it still felt like a confusing, incomprehensible space. Honestly, I still didn't really understand how I had cancer at all—the whole thing was oddly dissonant to me. Resistance was very challenging.

Chemo-resistance: literally my body resisting the medicine's healing effects. Fighting it, on some level. We talk a lot about fighting in the cancer realm. We are warriors, and we will fight this thing until we can't fight anymore. We battle our cancer until the end.

But battles and fighting have never been my shtick. I believe that violence begets violence, hatred begets hatred, battles beget more battles. Movements of nonviolence throughout history have always been the *fights* with which I have resonated. I have been deeply influenced, most prominently through spiritual community, by the philosophy of *active nonviolence*. Active nonviolence is an inner and outer gesture of non-harm. It is an idea that incorporates how we treat ourselves, our neighbors, our communities, and the earth. It is the empowered and embodied action of respect, listening, forgiveness, and reconciliation. Active nonviolence is all about experiencing and accepting dissonance and moving toward harmony. It is about shifting from resistance to collaboration—in strength, not passivity.

Being a battle warrior didn't make sense to me if this shift was the goal.

Were cancer and chemotherapy enemies that I needed to battle? Or was the fighting stance creating more fighting in the form of this resistance? How could my understanding of this trajectory toward harmony be applied in this situation? Could I collaborate with my treatment rather than resist it?

The cancer battle was bringing me down hard. But spiritual exhaustion can be clarifying—it forced me to step back and see what needed to change. This was the gift of chemo-resistance: I had to accept and surrender. And I had to shift from fighting to respecting, listening, forgiving, and reconciling. Rather than thinking of cancer as the enemy that I had to battle, I had to think of it as a displaced, confused friend who needed help. Like I needed to hug and hear the cancer, forgive it, and send it on its way. I needed a gesture of active nonviolence: *I'm sorry, cancer, but you're in the wrong place, and you really need to leave. I will stand here firmly and wait for your departure.*

It wasn't just the cancer that I had to stop fighting. The chemotherapy itself had become a poison that I was at odds with, that I was battling, too. The more I fought it, the more it fought me. I knew that the chemotherapy would need to be a part of my life for a while longer and that it would need my respect until it was time for our relationship to end. I had to say: *Chemotherapy, thank you for helping me. You are my helper. You are an intense and wacky sort of helper, and I forgive the ways that you mess with me sometimes. Let us collaborate to encourage our displaced friend, cancer, to move on out of here.* I know this might sound a little bonkers, but this was how I embodied active nonviolence in this situation.

I knew there were a couple of different options going forward, and that the likelihood of a cure was still very high even with the resistance. I was taking care of myself as well as I could, doing what I knew to do. So I had to stand tall, like the *Brightest Self Grown-Ass Woman Mother Tree* that I knew I was, collaborate with the chemotherapy to move the cancer kindly out of my body, and be patient with the slow movement toward harmony. I understand that not fighting cancer may seem like a radical idea. Take it or leave it, but in my experience, this mindset shift was liberating. I would learn more about the necessity of collaboration—personally and professionally—in my years of recovery.

Collaboration

Moving Toward Harmony

Turn on some music that will get you moving. You may not feel like moving much, but dancing will help to bring your systems into harmony. Try music that does not have words—I like a drumming track, personally.

Before you begin moving, decide on a goal for bringing about a more harmonious relationship:

- You might want to confront the cancer in your body. Bring to mind an image of your cancer. What does it look like to you? Have a little conversation with it: *Hey cancer, I see you. But you don't belong here, and it's time for you to move out. I am going to help you with this.*

- Or you might want to work with the chemotherapy that is in your body. Bring to mind an image of your chemotherapy: What does it look like to you? Have a conversation with it: *Hey chemotherapy, I see you. Let's work together for healing and non-harm.*

- You can also do this with any person, entity, poison, etc. with whom you are seeking more harmony.

Move your body as you imagine the cancer moving out. You may end up making sounds. That is a great sign that you are freeing yourself from inflexibility and harsh expectations. Keep moving as you are able, holding the image and the intent to harmonize.

Chapter Resources

Collaboration with Chemotherapy Meditation

This can be practiced while receiving treatment:

Tune into the chemotherapy that is entering your body. Take several deep breaths and simply become aware of it.

Visualize the chemotherapy as bright, sparkling light, filling your body with healing.

Breathe slowly and deeply as you continue to be held and healed by this light.

Repeat these affirmations to yourself or out loud as you receive your bright, sparkling treatment:

- *Thank you, chemotherapy, for your healing light in my body.*

- *My body and the chemotherapy work together to heal the cells that need to be healed.*

- *I welcome the chemotherapy as a bright resource for recovery, vitality, and wholeness.*

- *The light of chemotherapy helps my body.*

- *I am deeply relaxed in the knowledge that the harm of the chemotherapy is minimal.*

- *I believe in the light of this treatment to help my body recover, rebalance, and harmonize.*

Movement

The reality of chemo-resistance finally settled
in. I begrudgingly accepted this truth and began researching
various options for the next steps. Still trying to hold my internet
boundaries, I turned to the online forum to ask about other people's
experiences with second line treatment. They were mixed. Many
had eventually moved to an immunotherapy called pembrolizumab
(Keytruda). Several had raved about it, noting very few side effects.
They got their energy back, and best of all—it cured the cancer.
Many mourned that they hadn't been put on it sooner. How much
time in chemotherapy could have been saved?

Those who had not received immunotherapy had switched to
the next concoction of drugs: EMA-EP. The first three drugs (EMA)
would be the same, but the second week would be another dose of
etoposide (E) with the addition of cisplatin (P). I remembered my
experience with cisplatin from my induction phase and really did
not want to return to the platinum-based treatment.

I wanted the immunotherapy. It sounded like a dream to be
off chemo. Maybe I would get more energy and more hair. Maybe
I could begin to feel like myself. My friend Ferris was one of those
who found the immunotherapy to be curative. It felt like a very
hopeful idea to me, but my doctors were hesitant to go with it before
the standard second line chemo. EMA-EP was a successfully used,
well-researched option, and immunotherapy was still new for this

type of cancer. I sought a second opinion and was given the same advice: go with the second line chemotherapy. It has excellent success rates and would likely finish off my cancer fairly quickly.

But I was drained by the chemotherapy, by the entire experience—the cancer, chemo, the medical system, quarantine, the whole thing. Life at the farm continued to feel isolating. I still felt like a terrible mother. Surely, if nothing else, a break from chemo would give me the morale I needed to engage my life more fully. I had conversations with many people near to me, I prayed, meditated, I weighed the options seriously—and I decided that I was a grown-ass woman, and my intuition was telling me to give the immunotherapy a try. My doctors kindly, but hesitantly, agreed to the experiment.

⚬∞⚬

Mid-September. I sat in the chair at the cancer center for my first immunotherapy infusion, and my head spun. The nurse read aloud the long and comprehensive list of possible side effects. Immunotherapy could work wonders, or it could wreak havoc on my body in all sorts of ways that were *uniquely tailored to me*. It could cause my immune system to attack any normal functioning organ in my body, creating the possibility for virtually any side effect I could imagine. But I figured the side effects of chemotherapy certainly had to be worse than these possibilities.

The immunotherapy was quite different from the chemo. It took just an hour or so to receive the infusion, and then I did not need another for three weeks. Though I had heard such amazing things about this treatment, I was still nervous about a new medicine.

Based on my anecdotal internet research, it seemed like I could potentially go through nine to twelve weeks of immunotherapy and be done with the whole thing. The possibility of little to no side effects was appealing, and I was confident this treatment was going to help me. As I began, my hCG level was somewhere around 40. We had to get it down to 1.2 to be finished with this mess.

The nurse hung the bag of liquid medicine and I took a few deep breaths as I welcomed a new drug into my body. *Drip, drip, drip.*

I received my first infusion with no immediate problems. After waiting a couple of days wondering if I would start to get sick, I realized I had no side effects and was beginning to feel brighter. The fatigue lifted—along with my spirits—and my face de-puffed. This felt like a miracle after 28 infusions of chemotherapy.

For three weeks, I enjoyed getting back to life in a new way. I couldn't believe that I wasn't getting chemo; I had become so accustomed to spending Thursdays at the hospital. I had more time, more life, and felt myself liberated from the prison of poison.

I celebrated my 36th birthday, elated to have made it to this first week of October.

⚬◦

Three weeks after my first immunotherapy infusion, I arrived at the cancer center again with full confidence that this drug was working. I felt so good that there could not possibly be cancer in my body.

I checked in, got my blood drawn through my chest port. Then went upstairs and waited. After a long time, my phone rang, and I could see it was the doctor's office calling from right upstairs. Dr. Davidson was on maternity leave now, and standing in for her was a sharp and spritely red-haired physician named Dr. Haley Moss. She was calling with news I was not going to like (she told me this up front—Moss is a straight-shooter). My hCG had risen significantly, up into the 600s. She was not sure what to make of it. Sometimes immunotherapy makes everything a little worse before it gets better. She gave me the options: another round of immunotherapy and see what happens, or go ahead and move to the next line, the harsher chemotherapy. She recommended the chemotherapy, but reiterated that it was my choice. I deeply appreciated this as I wondered if Dr. Moss also stood in for Dr. D at the fancy dinner parties for beautiful doctors.

I had to decide rather quickly, but my gut was telling me to stay with the immunotherapy. I felt too good to question my original choice, my intuition—this *had* to work.

So I stayed at the cancer center, and I sat in the chair, and I got the immunotherapy dripped into my body through the robot chest box. And I felt good for another three weeks—lively and happy, relatively speaking. I could move myself in ways that I had not moved in so long. The experience of freedom and confidence in this treatment was deep.

A week after my second infusion I did experience one side effect: an ocular migraine (the circles in my vision), which I had not had since the early days of my cancer. This was odd, but mild on the scale of possible side effects and certainly mild in comparison to the effects of chemotherapy. I could handle seeing circles for an hour.

Later, I would learn that in my body, high hCG and ocular migraines were related.

⁓

While I was going through immunotherapy, my family took a "vacation" to an Airbnb on some beautiful land just twenty minutes north. I felt quite good during this time and finally had enough energy to take long walks again. I walked and walked, taking in the earth and the sky and the trees, enjoying the sight of barns and ponds. I could feel breath coming back into my body in a way that it hadn't in years. Elsie and Beatrice splashed in the hot tub and swam in the pool and we all enjoyed time away from home. We played games and watched movies, thankful for my time away from weekly treatment.

During this vacation, I had a consultation phone call with the Block Center. I probably did not need it—this was beginning to turn into a *too many cooks* situation. Despite my physical energy, I was feeling quite nervous after the first round of immunotherapy had failed to do what we hoped. I knew that it was a possibility that I would need to return to chemotherapy soon. I wanted to be prepared.

Though the nutrition part of the consult was redundant, the Block Center gave me tools for movement and resilience that I found greatly useful. The tools were in their book, but it was helpful to have their importance reiterated and a clear path laid out for me. I needed to exercise more and in more specific ways. My primary form of exercise at that point was walking, and this only happened when I had the energy. Thankfully, immunotherapy brought me back to movement and exercise, which stayed with me for the remainder of my treatment.

Life Over Cancer emphasizes the need for cancer patients to engage in a lot of exercise no matter what kind of treatment they are undergoing. Dr. Block speaks of *excessive rest syndrome* which can happen if cancer patients are ordered to prioritize rest during treatment by medical providers. When patients rest too much, they lose muscle mass, which is "the primary reservoir for glutamine, an amino acid that powers the anti-cancer immune defenses."[11] In other words, physical activity is of vital importance when going through cancer treatment because it uniquely keeps the immune system strong. A strong immune system is necessary for successful cancer treatment, as with healing any illness great or small.

The Block Center recommends a specific movement program for cancer patients, tailoring it to the circumstances of treatment. Their fitness regimen begins with the basics of postural alignment, engaging core muscles, and breathing properly. It moves on to whole-body conditioning, which includes a mixture of lengthening the muscles, strengthening the muscles, increasing endurance, and engaging in cardiac recovery exercise. They recommend at least an hour a day of a combination of these types of exercise.

I grew up doing gymnastics and practiced a lot of western yoga in my 20s, even completing my certification as a Registered Yoga Teacher in 2013. I have always loved to move in all sorts of ways, and most of these kinds of exercises were not foreign to me. I already enjoyed Pilates, and it checked the boxes for lengthening and strengthening. I was often trying to work on my endurance, running off and on throughout my life, walking briskly, or dancing. But cardiac recovery exercise was new to me, different from the HIIT workouts I had done before.

Cancer is an incredibly stressful event. The emotional toll is heavy, and the treatments are harsh on the physical body. It stretches and bends your spirit as if it were made of silly putty that is repeatedly run over by a monster truck. I had to nurture my ability to bounce back—to be able to return to that nice silly putty egg shape—in body, mind, and spirit. One of the ways we can do this is by intentionally putting ourselves in a stressful situation then teaching the whole self to recover. Cardiac recovery conditioning is a type of interval training that can accomplish this. The body will learn, over time, to recover more and more quickly. In my experience, this method works not only on the physical body but on the mind and the spirit, too. When we learn to recover the physical body from stress through movement, we build invaluable mental and spiritual resilience as well.

Movement is so essential for us as humans, whether we have cancer or not. Finding joyful forms of exercise will help motivate you to engage them. I know from experience how easy it is to fall into a rut and stop moving my body. I might always cycle through seasons of movement and stagnation, but I know how much better I feel when I stay active.

Movement

Find Movement that You Enjoy

Most importantly, find forms of movement that are fun and enjoyable to you. If it feels like torture it won't stick.

Block Center Cardiac Recovery Conditioning

You can use any exercise that you would use for endurance (running, brisk walking, biking, rebounding, dancing, jumping jacks, jumping rope, etc.).

Perform the aerobic workout for one to five minutes, followed by five to ten minutes of complete rest. Allow your heart rate to fully recover. This forms one set.

Repeat for a total of five sets. Ideally, these sets are done consecutively, but you may break them up over the course of the day if that is too much. Monitor your heart rate and aim for 50-60% of your maximum (your maximum is 220 minus your age) as the target during the aerobic workout. Do not go over 80% of your maximum target heart rate.

Feel Feelings

I traveled, once again, to the familiar Duke Cancer Center. I headed inside and straight back to the lab area to the left on the first floor. Three-needle poke into my chest port. Chit-chat with the port nurse. Blood drawn. It had all become so monotonous on one level. This time they wanted me to do labs the day before treatment—in case we needed to make a change—so I went immediately back to my parents' house to wait for the results.

I still hadn't learned how to wait for test results without tension. I sat on the floor in my parents' living room, trying to distract myself—which was all I could ever do when waiting for NEW TEST RESULTS.

My phone rang—by now I had learned that a phone call is not what you want. What you want is for the doctors to see the lab results and not be in a hurry about them. Sub-optimal results usually meant a phone call because something needed immediate attention.

It was Dr. Moss. "Hey Hannah, I have your labs here...umm...your hCG is over 4500. We haven't seen that number since late April."

My body sank—had I just lost six months of treatment progress? I felt like my insides were going to become my outsides. I could not keep doing this for another year. There was no way I would make it for that long.

It was still my choice, Dr. Moss told me, but she highly recommended that I start the second line chemotherapy. The dreaded cisplatin. Of course that was what I would do. I didn't even need to think about it this time—I knew it was the responsible decision. But it also felt like I was throwing in the towel: maybe I'm not a *grown-ass woman* after all.

I was crushed, actually. Cancer treatment had a way of flinging me around emotionally and spiritually, even when my physical self seemed to be doing okay. But this time the news hit me hard. The worst part was how deeply I was now questioning my intuition. *How could I have made such an error in judgment about my own health and body?* I thought I had made the decision to receive immunotherapy from a place of prayer and meditation and somatic awareness. *How could I have been so off?* I was flooded with shame and powerlessness—my Brightest Self withered with failure.

Experiencing myself as a *failure* was not new for me. I had been struggling to find my place, to figure out my meaning and purpose, for what felt like my entire life. I did not know who I was in the world. These were old stories, questions I had been asking myself since I graduated from college: *who am I? How do I fit in? What is my purpose?* My self-doubt seemed infinite. I didn't really experience myself as able to *do things*. I struggled with follow-through. It was a miracle that I had finished divinity school—I had thought about quitting thousands of times. I had attempted to start various small businesses when my children were young only to burn out before I even got them going. And I sure did not feel like an adequate mother or partner. I had tried belonging to various communities, and they were never quite right. My life felt like a series of failures—I felt the hit of one failure after another driving me down, making me smaller and weaker.

I don't think this experience is unusual for women in our culture, particularly in my generation. We hear a lot of messages that make it challenging to stand in our power. We were told, "You can do anything!" when we were little. What we absorbed was: "You have to do everything!" And when we can't do *everything*, we feel like we are failures. (I say *we* because I know there are a lot of us out there. I also know it isn't all women, and I hate boxes, but the collective *we* seems large enough to use *we* in this situation.) So many of us are swimming in the shame of failure.

Brené Brown says that shame is "the intensely painful feeling or experience of believing that we are flawed and therefore unworthy of love and belonging. We feel like something we have experienced, done, or failed to do makes us unworthy of connection." [12] That had been my experience: any failure felt like a flaw in my system. I had failed to live up to the expectations of other people—my family, my communities, my religion—and of myself. I routinely set goals that I could not meet. These failures made me feel flawed and unworthy of belonging, which made it challenging for me to connect with communities and individuals at a deeper level.

In that moment, this immunotherapy fiasco felt like failure. Failure on my part to hear the needs of my body. Failure to listen to the incredibly fierce and brilliant female doctors on my medical team. And it was a failure that could cost me my health, or in the most catastrophic of circumstances, my life. The stakes were high. The present-moment shame flooded together with the old, existing shame and I melted into a puddle of *failure* and self-resentment.

As it turned out, this welling up of shame was a huge gift. I was forced to begin a long process of releasing the shame in my body. It would be months into recovery before I would even realize how deeply it had taken up residence in my being. Of course, it wasn't the only emotion that I was holding tightly and needing to loosen. My fear was still intense sometimes, despite hard work to let it go.

I had thick grief that had been unattended. *Shame, fear, grief*—these three were enough to trap my whole self in stagnant wells of sludge at times.

⚬∞⚬

To begin releasing old emotions, the first step is to feel them. Sometimes it takes a triggering event—for me, the failure of the immunotherapy—to become aware enough to start this process. I was already prone to holding and stuffing down my emotions. I never knew how to express them well, so I had loads of them simmering in my system.

Cancer treatment will likely contain plenty of inflammatory occurrences. The nature of this experience is that it hits on all layers of the self—the physical, the emotional, the spiritual. Events will happen during treatment that will expose intense emotion, some of it old and connected to events from long ago. It might be uncomfortable, but you must give yourself permission to feel these feelings. This is work you must do within yourself, but it is also important to have at least one safe person who can be a holder of all the scariest things. It might be a therapist or a trusted friend. Maybe you have a family member who can bear to hold these feelings with you.

For most of my year in cancer treatment I continued to stuff my feelings in. I would have periodic meltdowns to people in my family—my only non-medical, in-person contacts—but they didn't even begin to scratch the surface. Beneath these meltdowns about my cancer treatment was a lifetime of emotions unfelt and unexpressed. This surface awareness was a strong first step.

The hope is to become more aware of emotions, so that eventually when they arise they will be felt and released in an ongoing manner. But first, any stuffed feelings must be brought to the surface and felt. Developing an awareness of the deeper experience and the web connecting present and past events and feelings will serve any person going through cancer treatment. From this awareness, release can slowly begin. Be gentle with yourself. Do this deeper work as you are able and have the energy for it.

Feel Feelings

Writing for Emotional Awareness

When you come to a moment that elicits a strong emotion during your cancer treatment, take the time to sit with it.

Grab a journal and write the name of the emotion at the top of the page (such as *shame, fear,* or *grief*). Start by writing as much as you can about the event that brought the feeling up.

Then, begin to move backward in time to the last moment when you experienced a similar emotion. Write as much as you can about this moment.

Move backward in time once more to another experience of this emotion. Write as much as you can about this moment.

Leave plenty of space in the pages that follow. Now that you are more aware of this emotion, other past events will start trickling in. If you can keep this journal handy, come back to the pages and write any time you remember another similar experience.

As these events are brought back into your consciousness, you will be able to see the web that connects them. Awareness of this web of relationships is necessary to begin the process of release.

Chapter Resources

Professional Help

If the emotions are too overwhelming or even incapacitating, a professional can be of great help in this process. I recommend an energy psychologist, a Somatic Experiencing practitioner, and/or a sound therapist who works with tuning forks. These modalities have been the most successful for me when my self-care practices aren't quite doing the trick.

Death

It was November. Beatrice turned three years old.

I worried about Beatrice, because she was too young to really know what was going on with me. It must have felt normal to her: Mom gets medicine on Thursdays and she gets to watch a bonus movie. Mom has weird hair and is tired a lot, so Esa takes care of her.

I didn't know how to help her feel and process something that she didn't know was happening.

Bea's hair was always a tangled mess. I sat behind this tiny person on the couch, and dowsed her matted curls in conditioner and coconut oil. I began to work on one section at a time with a comb. She gets extra Daniel Tiger while I do this—there is a lot of extra watch time these days, and I feel guilty about this, too.

It is very hard to untangle the tangles without hurting her; the balance is so difficult to strike. I just comb and comb, slowly. I have to use scissors to clip little bits vertically to break up the thickest knots. Hurting her is the absolute worst feeling. She yelps and her body tenses; so does mine.

But inevitably, something makes her giggle (usually Daniel Tiger). And that makes me giggle. So we get through the tangles, and all is well.

I combed for a couple of hours, rhythmically, meditatively. And the tears fell down my face. *What if I die? Who will get to comb her tangles out?* Other people would watch her grow and witness her journey of becoming, and I would miss it. She probably wouldn't even remember me. *Oh, how I ache to see her grow up.*

And so I comb, and she yelps, and she laughs—and I laugh, and I cry. She teaches me to untangle, to hold the laughter and the pain together. She is truly one of my brightest treasures.

Beatrice turned three, and she started school for the first time—mask-on, outdoor-only Waldorf school. Bea started school, and I started the next line of chemotherapy.

⚭

I began the EMA-EP. I dreaded the possibilities. Cisplatin (P), the platinum-based drug that can cause significant toxicity, frightened me the most. The first weeks of chemotherapy—so long ago now—had been distressing, and I did not want to go back. I did not want to return to blood transfusions or to that intense weakness in my body.

I also knew that I had resources that I did not have in those first weeks. I had the mistletoe, a solid nutritional plan, and various supportive supplements. I was exercising, meditating, and using sound. I had made it this far, intact in many ways.

When the first round started I was in an odd, complex state of fear and hope. It still felt like there could be a long road ahead. I did the math: if the progress was anything like my first line of treatment, then I could need six more months of chemotherapy. It was not math I liked, but I was trying to live in full acceptance of this possibility.

The hopefulness persisted through the first round, which brought my hCG down from 4500 to 168. I was elated. The second round brought it to 9.2. Still elated but getting tired and feeling the effects of the cisplatin.

December arrived. My third round brought my hCG to 3.8.

We moved from the farm to a neighborhood closer to the girls' school. The process is a blur to me, but our new space brought me out of isolation, which relieved a lot of stress—so much that I didn't even know I was carrying.

But I needed blood transfusions again, my platelets were taking a hit, and all of my blood work was starting to show deficiencies.

Christmas came and went, intermingled with cisplatin and with mistletoe.

Then it was January: a brand new year. 2020 had certainly been the strangest year of my life. What was 2021 going to be like?

COVID-19 vaccinations were beginning. The world was starting to loosen a little—a touch of light shining in the web of collective health fear. A subtle change was happening, and more was on the horizon.

All I could do was continue. I let others hold light and hope for me while I walked the path of spiritual exhaustion. I got my chemotherapy while the girls went to school, and we just kept going on this bizarre cancer and pandemic journey.

I finished my fourth round of the EMA-EP. The cisplatin was really starting to get a hold of me. I waited on my test results, hoping to Dear God that the 3.8 might be down to 1.2 so that I could just have one more round of this craziness and be finished. One more round felt like all I could possibly handle. I got my blood tests. I waited.

NEW TEST RESULTS arrived: 5.4.

My number had gone up. Though it was just a slight increase, I was devastated—spiritually ground to pieces and then pancaked. I desperately wanted to be done with this. I wanted to do something normal like teach math and spend long stretches of time with my children without wearing out. I wanted proper hair and I was angry that I even cared about hair at all. I wanted to have a Thursday that did not require me to be driven to the hospital and poked at. I wanted this robot box out of my chest. I wanted to feel like myself—though I wasn't totally sure what that felt like. It hadn't been something I had felt since college, since before the anxiety had set in. But I knew it was a possibility, distant though it seemed. I longed for connection and purpose in the world and felt like it might be within reach if I could just get through this cancer situation.

⤞⧕⧔⤝

I sat on the floor in the guest bedroom at my parents' house with my laptop. The girls were playing downstairs with their grandparents. I could hear them off in the distance, happy. After receiving these test results, I had a Zoom appointment with Dr. Davidson. Even on the screen she was put together, as usual. Beautiful, thick dark hair growing nicely out of her scalp. Alive and human and pretty. I missed having real hair and looking alive and human.

I sobbed.

"What part is making you feel the most upset at this point?" She asked, calmly and with genuine care. I gave it some thought.

"Well...I guess it's the fear that we are not actually going to cure my cancer. It's been so, so long now. It is getting harder and harder for me to do this. But if we don't cure it...I know that it's not the kind of cancer a person lives with for very long. I'm really, really scared that my children will grow up without their mother. I guess I am just still really afraid of death." More tears.

"Yeah...that's valid." She told me slowly and kindly, "That's really scary to think about." Dr. Davidson has two daughters, too. She knows.

I cried some more. We ended our Zoom appointment. I closed the computer and sat on the floor in stillness, feeling my feelings.

With these simple words, Dr. Davidson gave me permission to cross over a threshold into the darkness that I had not allowed myself to genuinely face. She told me my fears were valid and scary, and that was exactly what I needed to hear. Most of the people around me were excellent cheerleaders, and I usually needed them to tell me I would be okay, so they did. But I also needed to allow the emotions that come with unknowing. I needed permission to fear, validation that this was terrifying. I needed just a little external nudge toward the reality at hand— to go to the space where there is no light—down into the ground where death exists. I needed to experience the darkness of the soil.

I had to face the fear of death, and ultimately, I had to do it alone. For all the people who are cured of this cancer, there are still some who are not. I thought about how I might be one of those. *What would it feel like to really accept the possibility of death? Of early, tragic death, even?*

I lay on my back on the floor and let myself sink down low.

When I was nine years old we visited Grandmother Mary's gravesite. There were many of us there, though I can't remember who. We all stood and looked at the stone marking the life of the woman who had died so young and tragically. There was a stillness in the air, but it was speckled with Warner family chatter. I maintained silence, quietly staring at that stone with deep curiosity.

Something came over me in that moment, and I couldn't help but slowly walk closer. And closer still.

I lay down. Not on top but right next to where her body was put into the ground. Side by side, I felt myself sink into the soil.

Into the death, the sadness, the darkness. Into the earth with Grandmother Mary.

⌐⦚⌐

It is dark in the depths of the soil, and it is also full of nutrients. It is where death rests, and from where new life grows.

I had been grappling with my fear of death for years. Ever since coming near to it when I was nineteen, the possibility of dying young had terrified me. The ancestral story of my Grandmother Mary was deep in me as well. Those seasons in which I lacked meaning and purpose were particularly hard, and I was often quietly nagged by this feeling that I might—with a *poof*—disappear at any given moment. *Disappear to where? Leaving what behind?* These thoughts plagued me. *What is this terrible existence in which we are thrown onto earth without answers?* I hated not having answers. Surely there should be an answer for everything. My desire for answers had led me into studies of mathematics and theology—yet I had found in the depths of both subjects that the most beautiful concepts lie in the realm of the Infinite, the Mysterious, the Unsolvable.

⌐⦚⌐

I regained my composure after a half hour of crying. I walked carefully down the stairs, looking for the girls. Elsie sat alone on the couch. She also had a recent birthday and was six now. She felt older to me, not the tiny one she had been at the time of my diagnosis.

I sat down next to her. I held her close and felt feelings. I was still so raw from crying and it was evident on my face. She patted my cheek and asked me what was wrong.

"I am sad," I told her. "I am tired of being sick and getting medicine. I want to be better at taking care of you." My heart ached with this feeling of mother failure. It was still so strong in me, how badly I felt I was doing this job. And my spirit burned again with the idea of leaving the girls in this world without a mother, of not getting to watch them grow.

More tears trickled. I am never certain whether I am supposed to let my daughters see me cry or not.

"It's okay, mom." She said in her still-small voice. Elsie, my copper-headed child, has always had a depth of wisdom when she slows down enough to express it, and I could tell she meant it. *It's okay. All is well.* I gave her a weak, sad smile through tears and snot.

She spoke more truth as she touched my face: "We take care of each other."

Elsie is not my mother, and I know better than to put my care and emotional burdens in her little hands. But we do take care of one another in ways that are mysterious and sacred. We are souls journeying together. Her reminder of this brought the relief of breath and of vision to my whole self. She is another of life's brightest treasures.

I hugged her tighter, "Yes, we do. Always."

Some say the fear of death is the root of all fear; I think it is true. Our individual and collective fear stems from this deep anxiety, this tremendous discomfort with facing our physical mortality. We want to live forever, and we are not okay with the unknown. We go to great lengths to avoid death, believing it to be the worst possible outcome. Instead of facing it and accepting it as a beautiful Mystery, we fight it. We fight it, we fight one another, we do whatever it takes to live as long as possible. We collapse into ourselves as a means of preservation and survival. We distract ourselves from the pain. We turn away from joy because it is too hard to imagine it being ripped away by this greatest foe, death. Wouldn't everything be different if we were able to look death squarely in the eyes without fear?

Facing death was another long process for me. In the years that followed, I had to come to terms with how my fear of death was indeed the root of other fears I was carrying. I was afraid of all change, and I was also afraid of happiness. Both of these were the fear of death in disguise. My life reflected these fears, and there was a lot of work ahead.

Cancer forces us to face this reality of death. No matter whether the prognosis estimates many years of life or none, the word *cancer* is so strongly tied to death that we can't avoid addressing it. It can be uncomfortable to speak of it, but we must.

What if we could all sink deep into the depths of the dark soil and say *hello* to death? Breathe with it, laugh with it. Accept it— *really* accept it?

Death

Attend a Death Café

These are informal gatherings without a specific agenda. Their function is to simply bring the subject of death to the table, speaking and listening to one another. Speaking about it openly tends to be incredibly healing for most people, but take care of yourself while going through treatment and check in about whether it is going to be too overwhelming.

Local and online gatherings are listed at www.deathcafe.com.

Writing Prompt

Sit with your journal and consider how you think life would be different if the individual and collective fear of death no longer existed:

> *How would you feel? What would your day-to-day life look like? How would our communities function?*

Spend time in this alternate universe, taking note of what you see.

> *Are there any parts of this vision that you might begin to live out? If you were completely unafraid of death, what would you be doing right now?*

Chapter Resources

Practice Death

Lie down and listen to this meditative poem. Have someone read it aloud to you very slowly or record it for yourself.

To learn anything,

Practice.

Rest

In the palm of the earth.

Sink slowly, with roots.

Immobile with soil.

Decompose.

Fade to darkness.

To silence,

To release,

Float to sleep.

Practice death.

Shift your internal gaze

Upward.

To that which pours and streams

Through branches, leaves, and buds.

Immeasurable sky.

Light.

Feel the truth

In your Brightest Self:

Illumination is infinitely imminent.

Fire

February, 2021. I am with death—in the darkness, in the ground. I feel wretched.

⁓∞⁓

I had to get a lot of blood transfusions again, and I started developing antibodies to this blood. I wouldn't be able to receive much more. I was up to thirteen bags of other people's blood over the course of my treatment. I had been keeping count.

I took walks, but they were getting slower and shorter. Sometimes I got winded going up the stairs in my home. Hearing loss settled in, and they told me it would be permanent. The bottoms of my feet were numb with neuropathy. Chemo brain is real, and words got lost in the ether rather than coming out of my mouth properly. My funny hair was still growing.

My platelets had been teetering on the low end, so I began taking papaya leaf extract, which the internet said would be helpful. I went to acupuncture every week and to many other energy practitioners, too. My life was one appointment after another. I felt the weight of my health spending—all of my extra appointments and remedies were getting expensive, and it was stressful. I tried to enjoy the time I had with the girls, but my heart was weighed down. I was weary.

Yoga nidra and sound healing carried me during this time, as much as anything could.

I was getting puffier and more odd-colored. My eyebrows were almost nonexistent and my skin was rough and dry. Wispy hair poked out of the winter hat that I always wore. My appearance continued to disorient me, and I wondered if I would ever recognize myself again.

It had been almost a year of intense cancer treatment, so much longer than I had anticipated. Dr. Davidson told me to hang in there, that this is where it gets frustrating. *This* is where it gets frustrating?

I did more chemo math, and at this rate, there was no less than another month of chemotherapy. That was a hopeful number. I was not sure my body could stand up to another month of these poisons—if I would be able to *hang in there*. But there were no other options. Immunotherapy didn't work for me. I was trapped in the poison.

I am with death, in the darkness of ground—in the soil. There is not much light, but there are nutrients here.

I went in for my blood tests before the first half of my seventh round of EMA-EP. This time, they added another test to my regular labs: *hyperglycosylated hCG*. It was possible that the hCG left in my body was non-invasive and not actually harmful. This blood sample had to be shipped to an offsite lab, so it could take up to a week for results. We had done this test months prior when I hit the plateau—the test had come back positive then, meaning I still had cancer. I did not feel hopeful about the possibility of this test being negative. Hope was hard to reach.

Thursday, February 4th: time for my overnight stay at the hospital for my EMA infusions. I arrived at the hospital as usual with my rolling suitcase, pillow, and lamp in hand. A couple of nurses had taken to calling me *Lamp Lady*. I liked it.

I had started sipping on Gatorade (hospital options are soda, juice, Gatorade, or Ensure) during these past few treatments. In my pre-cancer wellness living days, I would have balked at the high fructose corn syrup and artificial color, but now I gave myself a little leeway. Every other week, while getting my overnight infusions, I would slurp on a little bottle of lemon-lime. It reminded me of my childhood—of my years spent in gymnastics, drinking blue raspberry Gatorade without thought of its ingredients. There was something very freeing about this indulgent addition. But it probably wasn't making me feel any better—wellness living makes some very good points.

My spirit was heavier, but the infusions proceeded as usual. I began to feel the familiar hollowness of the chemotherapy—*drip, drip, drip*— into my body as night fell and there was no longer light streaming through the little window. The machines made their *beep, beep, beeps*. I put on my eye mask and attempted to sleep, sleep, sleep in the windows of time between nurse visits.

In the morning, the chemo drip finished, and I took my steroids. Soon I would feel the weird energy that came with them. I packed my bag and gathered my things, said goodbye to the nurses, and walked myself down the hallways full of cancer-themed posters. I stepped into the elevator and undoubtedly made upbeat small talk with whoever else was there. I had a new batch of poisons swimming in my body, but maybe the people in the elevator didn't know how fresh it was. I had become a pro at faking cheerfulness with strangers.

My father picked me up in the drop-off circle. I was grateful to see him. He drove me to my house via the interstate—a shorter trip now that we had moved to Hillsborough. We were both worn down.

When I got home, I realized I had forgotten my lamp. It was okay; I would get it next time.

Four days later, the phone rang. I could see that it was Dr. Davidson calling, so I got nervous. This time she seemed happy, though. She told me in her factual yet upbeat way that my labs were back, and the special test had shown that my hCG was the non-invasive kind. I do not have any more cancer in my body. She wanted me to finish this round of treatment, and we would go from there. She had somewhere to be, so she had to get off the phone, but she wanted to give me this good news. She hung up, and I was left buzzing with this information.

Cancer-free. The news itself was stunning. *Cancer-free? My body does not have cancer? After all this time and all this heartache for everyone around me, I made it. Did I make it?...Maybe?* The news didn't settle in quickly. Like everything in this whole experience, it was abrupt, and it took me a while to process this new information.

But now I was even more sickened with the thought of going back for more poison in three days.

Thursday, February 11th. I arrived at Duke Cancer Center for my outpatient EP treatment. I got my labs through my robot box chest port. I chit-chatted with the nurse. I went upstairs to wait with all the other bald-ish people.

I got a phone call. *Ugh.*

It was a nurse from Dr. Davidson's office. My platelets were too low for treatment. I would have to go home, wait a few days, and then try again. She assured me that this happens regularly to cancer patients and that it was unusual that I hadn't had to deal with it yet. I guess the words were encouraging, but I still felt wretched—odd and achy, fragile in a way that I had not experienced since the beginning of this whole thing. I cursed the papaya leaf extract for being expensive and not as full of magic as the internet said it would be.

I went home, annoyed that I had traveled all the way to the cancer center and wasted my time. I felt terrible in my physical body, weak in my spirit, generally angry in my emotional self. I was so very tired, tired of being tired, tired of talking about being tired. *Just. So. Tired.*

I lay on the floor in the living room, next to the fireplace, where I often landed when I was alone. The girls were at school, Matt was working upstairs, and the house was quiet. I should have been getting chemotherapy at that moment, but instead, I was waiting for my body to give the okay. *How long would that take? And then what?* I would get the EP, the cisplatin. And I would feel even more horrible. I wondered if one bonus round of chemotherapy would be enough. I had heard from Ferris about extra bonus rounds. They did *not* sound fun.

I did more chemo math. Math has always had a calming effect on me (I know, it's weird). I started counting the weeks: *surely I am headed toward at least three more weeks of treatment, maybe five. Maybe more?* I would pass the anniversary of my diagnosis on February 24th. I will have done this for a whole year. *Is it time lost? How much time? Will this year have counted as living? Will I ever be okay after this? Is it even possible to feel good again? When might that happen? How many months or years? Will I develop a secondary cancer from all these drugs? Will I ever hold a job? Be a good mother? Will I feel the effects of this poison for the rest of my days? How many days will there be?*

And then I let all the thoughts fly away for a time.

I stared at the flames in silence. I felt the warmth of the fire, and for a moment I lost my worries to the mesmerizing color shifts taking place, the dance of heat.

My fire trance was interrupted when the phone rang. I could see that it was the doctor's office calling. *Oh no.*

It was Dr. Davidson, checking in on me after being sent home. How am I doing? *Oh, I'm swell. Peachy. So joyful.*

She began speaking slowly, with extra care—there was something in her voice that I could tell was more positive than usual. I had become rather adept at parsing out the vocal undertones of medical professionals at this point.

"Well, I've talked with a colleague at UNC," she told me. "And we have decided that you have had enough chemotherapy."

I heard it, and I searched through my muddled chemo brain for a response. It took some time for any sort of response to form.

"I have had enough? Like...I don't have to go back?...Ever?... What about bonus rounds?"

"You don't have any cancer in your body. You have had 22 rounds of chemo if you include the induction phase, along with two rounds of immunotherapy, and it's been almost a year. You have had enough. We will check your hCG again in a few days, and if all is well, we will keep a monthly eye on it. Does that sound good?"

Does that sound good? I wasn't actually sure. I was disoriented by this news. *She was telling me that I am released from the grip of chemotherapy?...Is that correct?* I had just been doing math and was trying to come to terms with a different schedule. I had to recalibrate.

"Yes...that...sounds...good." *Good* wasn't quite the comprehensive word for it. It sounded like a dream, like these words had come straight from dancing marshmallow angels with chocolate top hats. It would be awhile before I could believe it all.

We got off the phone and I sat with this unexpected news, just staring into the fire with it. I didn't tell anyone for a while; I wanted to be alone with this information. Eventually, I felt my whole self begin to settle in a way that it had not settled in so long. I let the salt water fall from my eyes. I allowed the twirl of flames to hold me, to receive some of the tension, the heartache, the grief. I felt the release of all the intensity that I had been holding for a year, and of other intensities that I had been holding for much longer. Not just a release from cancer, but other pain, too: the experiences of fear, tragic losses, other medical traumas, deep loneliness, shame, grief, fear and insecurity. I gave it all to the fire.

Like a controlled forest burn, just enough fire can rejuvenate the soil and improve the life of the trees. A balanced fire releases nutrients back into the soil and fertilizes the forest. I sat with the fire and felt a teetering toward renewal—just the smallest inkling. Held by fire at the end as I had been held by the Light in the MRI machine at the beginning. Fire is light, too: to move into the light of the sun is to move toward a hot, fiery ball way out in the cosmos.

Had I known that February 4th was going to be my last treatment, I would have brought cookies to the nurses and doctors. I would have said a hopeful goodbye to all these amazing medical professionals who had been part of this peculiar year. I would have ritualized that last stay in the hospital, taken a photo and high-fived the cement walls. Perhaps I would have remembered to take my lamp with me.

I like to think the lamp found a home on the ninth floor, that maybe it has lit the room for other cancer patients on their journeys. It is lovely to consider that as my work now: to take the light that softened the blow of my chemotherapy and let it illuminate the path for someone else. More likely, the lamp made its way into a storage room or the garbage can. But the metaphor stands.

It had been a month since I had spoken with Esli. With the intensity of the last weeks of my treatment, it was harder and harder to stay in touch. The last I had heard from her, she had stopped chemotherapy. She felt horrible, and her hCG levels were not improving much. The doctors weren't really sure why. She needed to listen to her body and stop the poison. She was praying for Divine healing for herself, and for me, too. I felt this.

February 4th was my last treatment day, and it was also the day that Esli died.

It would be a little while before I found out, and it was heart-wrenching news. I felt gnawing grief for her three little girls and her husband. Anger that healing had not come in the physical form. Guilt that I had survived, and she had not.

From the other side of the world, our little conversations had brought me peace and hope and camaraderie. Esli was surely a bright light for many. I thought we would be far-away friends for decades to come—that we would look back together on our coinciding journeys and speak of how rough that year was but how small in hindsight. Instead, our cancer journeys ended on the same day, in different, unexpected ways. Healing arrives in various forms; this I am learning. I will always carry her story with me, grateful for her light and her prayers, knowing that these continue beyond what we see in this life.

February 4th was a day of endings. They were abrupt, and they were also slow. These endings took different shapes— flames of the same fire, each morphing in their own ways. There is magnificent healing in the light of fire. The burning away of the old amidst the beautiful array of colors. Fire is more painful than the bright, calming light I had been visualizing. This closer, hotter light is more complex; and it is searing.

When it is time to release, the fire will be ready.

Chapter Resources

Fire

Fire Meditation

Light a fire, any (safe) fire: anything from a small candle to a big bonfire. Sit in front of it, and simply gaze at the flames. Allow yourself to be immersed in the colors and become mesmerized. Breathe slowly, and feel the release.

Expelling Fire Sound

In sound healing, the sound "haaaaaaaa" is associated with the element of fire. With gusto, make this sound 5+ times to balance the fire within.

Burn the Words

Take some time to thoughtfully write down experiences, emotions, and concerns that you wish to release. It could be just a few words or many pages. Spend time (a couple of minutes or many months!) meditating on these. When you are ready, create a fire in a fireplace or pit, allow yourself to meditate with the flames, and throw the pages in. If you can do this in a circle with other humans, all the better.

Breath of Fire with Retention

This is a variation of kapalbhati (breath of fire) breathing. Do not engage in this practice if you have cardiac problems, severe spinal issues, high blood pressure, or respiratory infection. Pregnant women should not practice breath of fire.

Chapter Resources

Find a comfortable sitting position with a long, tall spine. Rest your palms on your knees: face up or down are both fine, or if you would like you can touch your thumbs with your first fingers. Close your eyes and take a few deep breaths to center yourself. You will be breathing in and out of your nose for this practice.

Begin to take short, quick breaths through your nose.

When you inhale, you should feel an expansion in your belly area. When you exhale, you should feel a contraction in that same area. You can test this by placing one hand on your belly if you are unsure.

Make your inhale and exhale the same pace and equal length, but the inhale is passive, and the exhale is powerful. Place your focus on the exhale.

Do 27 breaths (27 inhales and 27 exhales), and on the last exhale, let all of the air out of your lungs, drop your chin and tighten your lower abdomen. Hold this for as long as is comfortable as you visualize a bright, fiery, colorful column of light in the middle of your body: beginning at your tailbone and extending all the way to the area above your head.

Take a long inhale and hold for 15 seconds, continuing to visualize the column of light. Then, exhale fully and feel the light move out of the top of your body into the infinite cosmos.

You have just completed one round. Begin again and work your way up to four rounds, for a total of 108 breaths.

Epilogue: Platinum

Down in the darkness of dirt, the critters crawl and the fungi eat death. The worms compost. I was still there, but the fire brought new nutrients, sparks of hope and potential. The chemotherapy was over, yet the journey was not. Recovery would be its own long, daunting process—a separate experience, in many ways.

The first thing I had to do was re-orient. I had to take stock of exactly where I was, come into acceptance, and surrender. I had to dig around in this dirt so that I might find clues that could help me on my way back toward sky.

I had spent the year just making it through each infusion, each test, each day. I had compacted my life into this medical form, and that is where I would remain for a while.

For most people with my particular cancer, a year of check-ups was normal. I would need two years because of my risk factor. This is peculiar in the cancer world, to not have to be under oncological care for the rest of my life or for at least a decade. So was the nature of this cancer: *peculiar*.

Returning to get my blood drawn and my hCG checked monthly was always a tense task. Four months into my recovery—just as I was about to get my port removed—my hCG number went up. It was alarming and exhausting, creating the need for scans, for a more careful watching, and the putting off of the port removal. I am still uncertain what happened—a few weeks later the number went back down.

They scheduled me to get the robot chest box removed in October, 2021. I spent nineteen months with the port in my body. I had grown used to it and the way it marked me clearly as a person going through intense medical treatment if my wispy hair and puffy face weren't automatic giveaways. But even as my hair thickened and my face took its usual shape, I still had the clunky box sticking out of my chest. To get it removed would be a sign of confidence from the doctors.

October came.

I turned 37, and I returned to Duke University Hospital to have the port removed under mild anesthesia. That day brought me back to painful memory—jabbed with needles in my arm again, lying in a windowless, sterile room again, people in masks poking at me—again.

The experience was nauseating, but the result was lightening.

⌒∞⌒

The roots of the trees pull the nutrients of the soil up into their trunks, branches, and foliage. Down in the darkness of dirt, the soil was rich.

I needed those roots—they would be my vehicle for growth back into the fresh air and toward the light of sun. The port removal marked the time when I turned my gaze toward the light enough to be able to look around and find these roots.

I had uprooted myself in so many ways. I was a Kentuckian living on North Carolina ground. I had undervalued my roots of place and land; I missed the Kentucky earth and the people from whom I drew my existence. I was far from home, continually trying to re-root. I was always digging around, searching for roots in the wrong places.

During my year of treatment, my maternal line had been loud. I had felt the ancestors and the Kentucky land through them in new ways. But the roots from my paternal side were different. My grandfather, the Baptist preacher turned pharmaceutical salesman, had died in July of 2020 at the age of 91. But in this strange pandemic time in history, it was like it hadn't happened. There had not been a real funeral and it felt deeply disconnected from my experience in North Carolina undergoing cancer treatment.

Grandpa Warner—Marvin was his name—was a fascinating, rough-around-the-edges kind of person. He built real airplanes in his basement and he seemed to love his dog, Judy, as much as (if not more than) any of his family members. He had been a redhead, like my daughter Elsie—though he went bald at a young age. He had freckly skin and sausage-shaped fingers. Grandpa ate crap and barked orders at people. He also made jokes and played the piano. He had remarried after Grandmother Mary's death, so Grandma Sharon was the only grandmother I knew on that side.

I had experienced the flashes of Grandmother Mary during my year of chemotherapy. I had developed a relationship with my dad's sister, Terry, and her husband, Chuck, during my year of treatment. Yet this section of my roots felt more mysterious: the Warners were loud in person, yet not as loud in my memory.

⌀

I continued to struggle with my spiritual-religious roots. My church upbringing, my experience in divinity school, and movements in and out of church structures all left me still wondering whether I belonged in this space at all. But these were roots I could not ignore, uncomfortable as they were sometimes.

I needed to go back even further, deeper into the roots of the Christian worlds, to a spirituality of depth, connection, and hope. There are mystic strains of Christianity—those ancients who experienced God in various, sometimes intense ways. The mystic traditions spoke to me in a way that other forms of Christianity had not. I turned to a spirituality that would allow me to question. I had to give myself permission to find this expression of faith that was different from my roots in many ways. I became more open to the Mystery of God and of life. I started to see that there are layers upon layers of experience, shifting states of consciousness, and an expansive cosmic force of energy from which we draw our life and our experience. The Christian narratives offer me a sense of tradition and holding. I also needed to connect with people and ideas from different spiritual backgrounds. All of this became crucial for my healing process.

Digging into the roots of my existence—into the stories of place and of people—brought me into a state of openness to something bigger than myself, to the potential of a larger story unfolding. Throughout my entire cancer journey, I felt the prayers of others as incredibly real and authentic. They held me when I was powerless and small. I felt the prayers from Kentucky family and friends as especially potent, and it was through these roots that I was able to draw nutrients from the soil. By beginning to embrace where I came from, I started to grow in new ways—in the direction of an infinite Source. Like a strong Mother Tree, I allowed the roots to hold me steady while the nutrients began to seep upward toward new growth. There was possibility and potential; I could feel it welling up inside of me by the end of 2021.

⸎

I continued the slow crawl upward toward the spaciousness of air. *Smotherhood* had been lifting throughout this whole process, but now there was really life ahead—growth and movement. There was brightness on the path and I experienced it intensely. I felt myself float a little more, become a little lighter. I became stronger in my self. Laughter and play returned. Celebration and peace, too.

The monthly checks continued. I still hated them. I grew dizzy every time I saw that email with the subject line NEW TEST RESULTS. But relief came a little bit at a time—month by month. I returned to work part-time, tutoring math students at the Waldorf school. I developed confidence in my ability to do things again.

It was a lot of work to process the medical trauma: I went to therapy, did a brain retraining program, got a stellate ganglion block shot for PTSD (I am still not sure if it was helpful). I did math again, which brought me out of my emotional brain in an oddly therapeutic way (I recommend KenKen puzzles). I decided to become a proper Waldorf teacher and attend training when the summer of 2022 arrived, a year and a half into my remission.

⌒∞⌒

Waldorf teacher training was like a healing retreat for me: two and a half weeks in July in beautiful New Hampshire with other adults learning the basics of the pedagogy. This included painting, singing, movement, and study, so in contrast to weekly chemotherapy, it was a vacation. It was by far the longest amount of time I had spent without my children since becoming a mother, and I missed them but also felt how important it was for me to do something toward my professional, outside-of-the-home development.

I stood in a circle with seven other women, singing in harmony with our strong and beautiful leader, Meg. Her voice is powerful, and she held the space for the rest of us to find the strength of our own voices. I hadn't sung with other people in so long—I couldn't even remember the last time. For all the ways I had been using sound throughout my treatment, I had not been singing like this. I had not experienced this kind of harmonic goodness since I was a child in choir.

Sisters come and gather near me
Circle round the sacred well
Sing a song we'd nigh forgotten
Tell the tale we've longed to tell.[13]

In another class we seeped ourselves in color, painting simple forms with watery paint. I had found a love for painting in college, but it, too, had fallen out of my life. Being with the color, allowing creativity to flow again, brought more healing.

I wrote in my journal that I felt like myself again, for the first time since I was nineteen. This was no small moment. There were so many bits that coalesced that summer at teacher training: I had taken a trip by myself with high nerves and other symptoms of post-traumatic stress, and I had completed the task with flying colors. I got to interact in profound ways with caring, fascinating adults. I experienced professional purpose. The artistic activities were deeply nourishing. My Brightest Self finally broke free and I began to come alive again.

⌒◇⌒

August 2022 arrived. My teaching journey continued. I began the academic year as the middle school math teacher at the Waldorf School—a return to the job I had left abruptly with my cancer diagnosis. I enjoyed being there, with students and colleagues and numbers and shapes. It was a vast improvement over hospitals and poison drips.

It was time for my monthly blood test. I was still nervous, but I was now 18 months in remission. I was counting down the months until I would be released from oncology—six more after this. Six more monthly checks, six more emails with NEW TEST RESULTS.

Epilogue: Platinum

How would I feel when this was over? Liberated? Would this experience ever really be over?

I checked in at the cancer center. Got my blood taken through my arm since I was port-free. The nurse slipped the needle in easily; I was relieved. I made my way upstairs to the waiting room. It was such a routine, and I knew it would be a routine for a while longer. I ached for freedom from these appointments.

They called me back into a patient room. Matt was with me. The room was windowless and cold, but somehow I had grown comfortable there. We chatted with the nurse happily—everything looked good. Labs were fine and I was healthy. More waiting.

Enter Dr. Davidson—*click, click, click*—put together, kind and direct as usual. She reiterated that everything looked good. We talked for a while. I asked her about her daughters; she asked me about mine. I wondered to myself what she was going to eat for dinner. Maybe she would have a dinner party with Dr. Moss. Fancy wine glasses and fur coats—hearty laughter. Dr. Watson would have been there, too, but she had moved on to a different hospital and city.

"Well, I don't think I need to see you anymore," Dr. Davidson said matter-of-factly. I snapped out of my daydream.

By now we all know that I do not process these bits of information quickly. I struggled to find a response, again.

"What? What do you mean? I thought you wanted me to come in monthly until the two-year mark?"

"You're doing great. I think you're fine. Call me if you have any symptoms." I was confused.

"...that's it? Like...I don't have to come back?...Ever?" So many thoughts swirled in my head about what this could possibly look like.

"You don't have to come back. Go live your life."

My life? My life. I get to have a life?...I get to have a life.

She hugged me, and I thanked her for her care, but I was stunned again. She walked out. And that was it. It's like the universe doesn't want me to bring people cookies! I am happy to be released...I think.

Like this whole journey—the abruptness was fitting. All I could do was go live my life, like Dr. Davidson said.

⁙

My life was teaching math for a couple more years. Into studies of Waldorf mathematics curriculum I twisted and turned. I was led into the Quadrivium—number, geometry, music, and cosmology, which took me into the mathematics of frequencies and the spirituality of sound. Mathematical beauty—in forms visible and invisible—is all around us. I found tuning forks to be a fascinating combination of mathematics and healing, and I learned to work with them on myself and others.

Music found me again. For most of a decade the only music I had been listening to was pretty awful children's music. I don't know how this had happened—for I have always been an avid lover of music. I began to sing all the time—with students in my classes, with friends, with my kids, and in the car with myself. My spirit was able to find joy in ways that had been lost for so long. Those near me heard a lot of the *Appalachian Round*:

> *Take me back o hills I love*
> *Lift me from this lonely bed*
> *Light my way with stars above*
> *Curl soft winds around my head*
> *Wash my feet in crystal streams*
> *Cradle my arms in boughs of oak*
> *Breathe the scent of pine for dreams*
> *Wrap me tight in earthen cloak* [14]

⁙

More change would come as I made the identity shift from *patient* to *healthy human,* as I learned what it was like to be *myself* again. I completed training as an end-of-life doula, I went to Waldorf teacher training for another summer. I returned to childhood loves of roller skating, Appalachian clogging, and acrobatics—I learned that a grown-ass woman can also be curious and playful. I quit teaching in hopes of supporting others and myself in a different way. My life shifted drastically in many realms.

∞

It was time to tell the story. We all have different ways of storytelling; it doesn't have to be a book-writing project. It might come in the form of visual art, of music, of words spoken to a friend. The audience need not be large, but it might be. You will know when it is time to tell the story of your experience with the poison. It is a vital process on the journey of recovery.

∞

August, 2023. Amid this writing project, I felt drawn to visit Kentucky. I called my mother, who loves a good, long drive: "Do you want to go to Kentucky tomorrow?" She did. So we went to Kentucky the next day.

We visited the land that used to be my grandparents' farm. I hadn't been there in fifteen years.

It was different, yet the same. The barns were all intact, the house looked as I remembered it. But the 180 acres were covered in GMO soybeans, likely sprayed regularly with glyphosate. The realities of the agricultural industry in rural eastern Kentucky settled in. I had grief. And hope, too, somehow. We drove around the land and I hopped out to take photographs at every turn. We arrived at Papaw's barn.

I entered it alone. The dirt floors were as they had been when I had last visited. I lay down in the middle and absorbed the faint scent of tobacco and tractors—it still smelled the same, too. Down in the dirt I sank. I closed my eyes, and tears streamed down the sides of my face. I felt Papaw's presence and A.A.'s, too. And Robert and Marilyn and all those who had made this place what it used to be.

My eyes flittered open, and I looked to the sky that trickled in through the barn panels. Streams of light shining through the cracks—here in the dark, in the dirt.

⁓✧⁓

The last stop was to visit my climbing tree—*Hannah's tree.* I wondered if it would look big and strong, like the Mother Tree I was striving to be. Surely much the same as it was, but I imagined there might be more foliage and stronger branches.

Hannah's tree was still there.

But it was different.

It looked to be...smothered, on one hand. Big chunks of another tree had fallen on it, vines were climbing up and around the trunk and winding all around the branches. The big limb I always used for dismounting my tree was dead.

Several other little trees were growing up and out from the bottom—separate ones of a different species. And they were thriving. My tree appeared to be feeding these other trees—nourishing them, helping them grow. Overall, my tree was strangely thriving, too. I looked up and saw that it was growing tall and strong. It had foliage despite all these happenings all over it. It continued upward toward the sky—toward light and breath.

My mother and I stood together, in perplexed awe.

This was my story.

⁓✧⁓

Cisplatin: the platinum-based poison that wreaked the worst havoc on my body. It was the one I feared and dreaded the most. The thought of it still makes me feel a little frail.

Platinum is a precious metal. It is stronger, denser, and more durable than gold. The form of platinum in my chemotherapy was different from the bling on your finger, yet the basic substance is the same. Deep in the grossest poison, there was something of worth.

In order to move forward, engaged in life, I had to take stock of these most valuable bits of my experience. I had to hold them tight and allow them to transform me, then share the resources I found and continue along my journey in confidence.

Smotherhood, it turns out, was not an indictment of motherhood at all. It was about the internal pressure to be all things to all people, my children included. It was about my own lack of vision and self-imposed limitations.

The poison of smotherhood found its remedy in the platinum of empowered storytelling, of sound and music, of creative expression and the sharing of resources. The antidote to being smothered was to find my voice, and I only found it by going through this poisonous journey. The Platinum is the ability to stand tall and strong as a Mother Tree—a grown-ass woman who is her Brightest Self.

Parenting is still hard; it will never be easy, and I wouldn't have it any other way. Sometimes it completely wears me down, sometimes I use my *frustrated voice*. Our society does not equip mothers well— we are parenting in isolation, stretched in a thousand directions at the same time. I have had to learn to accept help and to surrender. I try my best, and that is good. Parenting is about growing toward the light, roots intertwined with my daughters. My job is to model the finding of purpose and creativity and health and community, empowering them to do the same. I want my children to be able to speak their truth in the world with strength, too. Parenting is a quiet but extraordinary task. It is the task of turning my children's gazes toward the sky, toward the sparkling expanse of the Cosmos. To help them find their breath, their air. My daughters will not choke; they will sing. Of this I am determined.

Elsie and Bea, Elsie and Bea, Elsie and Bea. They turn my eyes toward Light, too—in ways that I can now see clearly but that I could not see before. Elsie and Bea—the Sun and the Moon—a vision of a balanced Sky.

I am forty now. Motherhood did not kill me, neither did it kill Grandmother Mary. Words spoken can have such an impact on us, and I am learning to take Dad's musings with a grain of salt. Motherhood—and the cancer that came from it—forced me to heal old patterns in ways that I was unable to access before. *The truth is that motherhood saved my life.*

When you finish treatment, be kind to yourself—value yourself. You won't be the person you were before. There are growing pains; the healing process is complex. Whether you have lingering side effects in your physical body (I had neuropathy for a year, permanent hearing loss, and my hormones were wrecked), are struggling with symptoms of post-traumatic stress, or look up and see that big things in your life need to change, you have permission to be a different human. Going through this toxic treatment is a huge event. Be gentle with yourself as you navigate a new way of being.

After a challenging experience, we get to make a choice. We can let it crush us and allow ourselves to be victims of our hardships—or we can lean into our power and choose to walk forward in hope. I had to acknowledge my grief about the whole situation, and also stand strong with the gifts from my year of treatment.

Once you have been through chemotherapy, you are part of a group of people who have experienced something intense and medically atypical. It's not the club you wanted to belong to, but it's the one you are stuck with. We are better able to move forward in recovery when we support one another and collaborate, when we share our resources. Our stories, lessons, ideas, recommendations, and questions are our greatest gifts from the journey.

~∞~

The term *alchemy* is an old one—classical alchemical texts refer to the mixing of ingredients as the precursor to modern chemistry. These ingredients are not simple—everything material has a corresponding spiritual resonance. Through the mixing of spiritual-material substances, a transformation will occur—the expression of something new through images, words, sounds, and symbols—a divine unfolding of new life. Alchemy is about engaging with the substances and the processes in this interwoven spiritual-material realm that we exist within.

~∞~

I began with poison. The poisons were many—they were cancer and chemotherapy, fear, shame, grief, and isolation. Slowly, the poison mixed with the light, creating circles with specks of dust. Energy and restoration were added to the concoction—and a hint of the Brightest Self appeared. Sound and nourishment from the earth brought growth, webs began to strengthen. Mistletoe added strength and peace. Laughter brightened the blend. Water brought cleansing and fluidity, collaboration triggered movement. Big feelings broke through, and all of the ingredients sank into the soil, with the fire. The poison began to transform. The bits of platinum that were glittering in this mixture became shinier and shinier until they illuminated a new, brighter form. Somehow, in ways more Mysterious than not, I was healed by poison.

The alchemical symbol for Platinum is the Sun and the Moon together. Platinum represents totality and vision. It nudges us toward brightness and darkness, toward the conscious and the unconscious, toward activity and rest. It symbolizes a balanced sky—an infinite expanse of potential. The Platinum is the greatest resource, found in the depths of the poison.

When we traverse the layers of our most challenging experiences—when we open ourselves to growth and Potential—we will always find something bright and valuable buried within.

There is meaning in the muck.

There is substance in the sludge.

There is treasure in the toxins.

There is Platinum in the Poison.

Postscript

You don't finish things, they tell me. These words have been spoken by too many people in my life, and they are biting.

I have started businesses, have numerous pieces of unfinished art lying around, I am divorced. I am no longer a math teacher and I did not complete my Waldorf teacher training.

What does it mean to finish something?

My manuscript neared completion, having been through a couple of rounds of editing. But I was nagged by these questions: *Who is this Grandmother Mary? Why are there such parallels between my story and hers? Why has the story of her life been so quiet? How are these wounds affecting my entire extended family, even 52 years after her death?*

We are all holding the experiences of our ancestors up to three generations back within the makeup of our DNA— I am certainly not the only one with a harrowing tale from the past. There is plenty of research out there in the field of ancestral trauma.

I felt these questions so profoundly that I considered a complete addition to this book, but it was going to take months or even years to adequately address them. I decided, instead, to *finish* this project as I had planned.

⌗

I have begun taking walks at a farm park nearby. It used to be a family farm, and now it is a park with walking trails and picnic tables. It is made up of woods and fields and a nice-sized pond. There is still a barn and an old house on the property. It is too close to the interstate for my taste, and the zooming of the cars can always be heard in the distance, but the visual of it is very Kentucky-esque. North Carolina and Kentucky don't look the same: the trees are different and the hills don't roll here quite the way they do back home. The grass is a different color. Both places are beautiful. I have taken to walking or jogging at this park because it reminds me of my roots.

After months of spending time in this place, I finally noticed a sign: *Mary's Trail* and *Alice's Loop*. Two trails, with my two grandmother's names, pointing in different directions, on the same sign. One afternoon I walked the grandmothers' paths as I talked on the phone with my Aunt Terry, my dad's sister. Aunt Terry and Uncle Chuck were with me during my cancer treatment via many, many phone calls. Chuck went through chemotherapy years ago and they were a great support to me on this journey. But we hadn't spoken in a while; life happens.

"Tell me some stories about your mother." I asked of her. It was so odd how few stories I had heard. I could always feel how much pain was there for my dad and for his siblings, but that generation doesn't talk much about their emotional experiences.

Terry told me stories of Mary. How she was fun and lively and loved to dance and play music when she was healthy. How she had not liked being a pastor's wife. How the medical system had given her drugs to treat what they diagnosed as manic-depressive disorder, and in many ways the drugs made things worse. How she was uncomfortable in her marriage and felt isolated as a stay-at-home mother. How she had just started business school the year she died, thinking that getting out of the house would be helpful for her health. Aunt Terry had been told that Mary was never the same after a bout of whooping cough when she was a child.

So much of this story felt familiar to me. What would it take for these wounds to mend in our family system? What would be the outcome, if we could move toward a deeper level of healing?

Aunt Terry recalled their last family vacation together. Mary and Marvin with the four kids at the beach: Michael, Terry, Rick, and Tammy. Mary secretly smoked cigarettes—by 1972 it was shameful in the circles where she roamed. But she pulled out a cigarette on the beach, all the kids and the husband sitting there, and she smoked that thing. Aunt Terry said she was thinking *you go, Mom.*

Mary smoked a cigarette, and maybe for a moment she was liberated from all of these hardships. Maybe it was her cigarettes that freed her from smotherhood.

Death brings liberation, too. And pain.

Was her life unfinished?

I have come to believe that time is way more complex and interesting than we think it is. My life has unfolded exactly as it needed to—these *unfinished* bits serve as preparation. Sometimes programs or projects don't get *finished* because they must transform into something else. Sometimes we don't meet our human goals because the broader experience of life happens to be way more interesting than that. I return, over and over, to the many resources I have gathered these forty years. Time shape-shifts experiences into new forms. Those *unfinished* things aren't unfinished at all. Change is the only constant: this I learned from Calculus (and from Octavia Butler). To live in fluidity with life's most certain waves of death is to live in spiritual peace.

I have finished this book, in a sense. The words are set as they are now, and I can't do anything about it. But the story continues; the end isn't really the end at all. I have learned to get comfortable with the Mystery of eternal questions and unfinished dreams.

Now I walk the Grandmothers' Paths, curiously toward the next chapter.

Platinum, 2023.

Who would we be if we weren't afraid of death?

If together, we traveled through portals shallow and deep.

If we came out of them knowing the depths of our own spirits: that we are eternal. Infinite beings.

That Love transcends time and space.

Without death's grip, all fear would evaporate. It would float from us in tiny particles, out and away to be devoured by the sun.

Perhaps, then, we would be able to see. Look away from our screens. Into one another's eyes.

To earth and to sky, to moss and fern and fungi.

We would sit together, in woods and in fields, in rain and in light. We would stroll barefoot into forests. Holding the hands of friends who aren't even lovers.

We would laugh. Until we fell over, healed.

We would dance, climb, and spin. And fall again.

We would make sounds: song and rhythm and words. With mouths and hands and hearts.

Could we be silent, then?

We would cry in circles, around fires. We would groan with the grief of the world, hold the sorrowful breath of the ground, and then we would scream and let it burn. And laugh and start over.

I suspect, if we weren't afraid, we would walk away from the scrolling and checking to gaze at the blue light of the moon.

We would feast at large tables and hold and hear differences. Forgive these variations.

Melt our weapons and resurrect them into art.

We would float down gentle streams of change and allow ourselves to be placed on new land with joy.

We would love our decaying bodies, one another's decaying bodies.

Bathe ourselves in color and let it emanate from our limbs. Into the air. Into the souls of our neighbors.

Without fear, we would work, and we would rest. In balance and in harmony.

We would release our excess to the trees, who are good at recycling.

Would we listen to questions? And ask them with courageous curiosity?

We would sit quietly with one another, in awe of the Mystery of our limitless, liminal existence. For there is enough time.

We would make circles upon circles. Through portals we would go. Toward Light, toward Enigma, toward Boundless Love.

If we didn't fear death?

We would breathe. We would wait.

Then perhaps we could be ourselves: Human.

Appendix: The Recovery Spiral

Obviously I love circles. You will need a circle to engage the work of recovering from chemotherapy—this is vital. But the *process* is not circular or linear (neither is it a square, triangle, or hexagon). I think the path to recovery is a more of a spiral than anything else—a golden spiral, in particular (it gets more and more open as it gets larger, with a growth factor of *phi*). In my experience it involves nine processes. The goal is to move toward more and more days of feeling bright, alive and engaged with life. There will always be hard days, and recovery will likely never be complete. The experience is in us now, but we get to choose how to hold it as we move forward. The following are the nine processes toward physical, mental and spiritual recovery from chemotherapy or any challenging experience that life may present.

Engage Life
in Clarity and with Purpose

Gather Resources
for Growth

Share Your
Resources

Explore Your Roots

Rest + Reorient

Name the Value
of Your Experience

Embrace Potential

Tell Your Story

Nourish Your
Brightest Self

Notes

1 Watson, Bruce. *Light: A Radiant History from Creation to the Quantum Age.* (Bloomsbury USA, 2016), xiv.

2 If you would like a more comprehensive understanding of this practice, I suggest *The Heart of Centering Prayer* by Rev. Dr. Cynthia Bourgeault.

3 Delafield, Martha. www.marthadelafield.com

4 Gach, Michael R. *Acupressure's Potent Points: A Guide to Self-Care for Common Ailments.* New York: Bantam, 1990.

5 Some of this practice is based on the scripts from Swami Satyananda Saraswati's book *Yoga Nidra* (Yoga Publications Trust, 1998).

6 Turner, Kelly A. *Radical Remission: Surviving Cancer Against All Odds.* New York: HarperCollins, 2015.

7 Keyes, Laurel Elizabeth. *Toning: The Creative and Healing Power of the Voice.* (Camarillo, CA: Devorss & Co, 2008), 49-61.

8 Gaynor, Mitchell L. *The Healing Power of Sound: Recovery from Life-Threatening Illness Using Sound, Voice, and Music.* (Boulder, CO: Shambhala, 2002), 153-4.

9 Spitulnik, Debbie. www.theartofspeech.org

10 Cowan, Thomas. *Cancer and the New Biology of Water.* (Chelsea Green Publishing, 2019), 35-46.

11 Block, Keith. *Life Over Cancer: The Block Center Program for Integrative Cancer Treatment.* (New York: Bantam, 2009), 158.

12 Brown, Brené. "Shame vs. Guilt." January 15, 2013. https://brenebrown.com/articles/2013/01/15/shame-v-guilt/.

13 ODell, Meg. *Gather.* www.singwaldorf.org

14 *Appalachian Round,* traditional.

Acknowledgments

It is absolutely, infinitely impossible to acknowledge all the people who have supported the writing of this book. It is a lifetime of individuals and communities who have given me the fodder I needed to complete this task.

Of course I begin with my parents, Lisa and Michael—who brought me into this world on the 2nd day of October, 1984.

I am especially grateful for the birth pains of my mother and their continuing call for me to grow. For her intuition and her wisdom, for her genuine care for others—I am thankful. I will never know all that she did during this year of chemo, but I saw childcare, foot rubs, a thousand meals cooked, three thousand dishes done, seven thousand errands run. She maintained calm and peace when I was not calm or peaceful, she encouraged me, and she prayed actual prayers. She is Superwoman.

I believe our families of origin provide the content that we are meant to work with for the rest of our lives for our greatest spiritual growth. Since I also believe that the deepest value lies in our biggest challenges, it is not surprising that we often have at least one parental relationship that is a source of struggle. In truth, my dad and I have had difficult seasons. We see the world very differently; and we are both stubborn. And I know he loves me beyond words, and I felt his fervent prayers during this year of chemo and always. I am truly grateful for all the resources he has provided over the years— for the many, many forms those resources have taken— and for being the first one to read this book in its entirety. I think my dad is awesome, and he's challenging sometimes (surely he would say the same of me). He points me to the places that need healing. He teaches me to love beyond incredible ideological disagreement, and that is a worthy lesson for our times. Michael is exactly the dad I needed in order to be the person I am becoming. I am truly grateful.

I am thankful for Claire, my sister, who continues to amaze me as I watch her becoming a mother. She is the greatest aunt and provided countless hours of kid-care and personal support during the year while navigating immense challenges as a teacher during the pandemic. Thank you for sitting with me during chemo and for loving Bea and Elsie so well.

Matt, my co-parent, was graciously supportive on this journey. He cared for our children and the home with gusto. His presence is not often found in these pages, as our stories of our time together veer in wildly different directions and this book is not about that. Marriage is no longer our relationship, but I see clearly the support that he offered over the years. I am grateful for him, and I am glad our daughters have him as their dad. Matt's parents, Mo and Phil, offered invaluable support by way of medical advice and cheerleading throughout the year.

I'm especially grateful for the people who showed up at the ER that day in February. Beyond my family, that group included Leland Rayner, Maureen Welch, Megan Pardue, and Leah Wilson-Hartgrove. And to those people who showed up at the hospital in the days and weeks following—Jonathan Wilson-Hartgrove, Sarah Jobe and Shana Bertetto in addition to the ER group. (As an aside: yes, every time I write *ER*, I do see George Clooney's face. I am a child of the 90s, after all.)

The web of love stretched so far beyond the people who were there in person. My whole extended Kentucky family are the best pray-ers a girl could ask for. But there are so many of them. So, to all the Gardner-Hinton crew, to the Warners and the Gusslers, thank you for the love and encouragement. There aren't words that capture the feeling of being held from far away. It is magic. My cousin Sarah Hinton set up a Go Fund Me, and I am immensely thankful for this and for the 116 contributors that supported my family during this time. The website will no longer allow me to access that list of people, so I apologize for the lack of proper *thank you* cards.

I am grateful for the ancestors whose presence is not lost: Alice Gardner, Elgin Gardner, Robert Kinzel, Marilyn Kinzel, Mary Dunlap Warner and Marvin Warner.

Others in Louisville were also holding me and sending love— notably my mom's besties (Laurie Oliver and Sherri Romano) and her circle of people (which includes any person ever affiliated with Second Presbyterian Weekday School). I am grateful to Raleigh Langley and the folks at St. Francis, as well as college and high school friends who reached out.

I am grateful to the communities I have been a part of since moving to North Carolina: friends at Duke Divinity School, at the Rutba House, and those I met during yoga teacher training. The Emerson Waldorf School contributed deeply to my recovery in my years as a math teacher. Students and colleagues challenged me, made me laugh, and brought new resources for growth into my life. The folks at Waldorf teacher training brought a great deal of spiritual development in just two short summers, and there was much beauty and learning in this time.

I had the three most fantastic doctors: Dr. Brittany Davidson, Dr. Catie Watson, Dr. Haley Moss. And Dr. Allison Puechel, who was only there for a moment but also amazing. I can't say enough about my medical team and the incredible love and brilliance of these women (and Dr. Harris, too). I am so grateful for their strength and wisdom, and I hope they get to take a break and have a fancy dinner party every now and then.

I couldn't have made it through chemotherapy without the additional support of my integrative team: Dr. Dave Allderdice, Dr.

Renee Meyer, Ian Florian, Martha Delafield, Robin Whitlow, Mary Justus, Jill Beck, and Sarah Young. I am grateful to Viorica Comaniciu and Sally Whitaker for the outdoor walks which provided additional health and sanity.

If we crossed paths at all in my life then you likely contributed something to my growth, which directly affects my writing. I am grateful to the community in Richmond, Kentucky where I began my life's journey—the nourishment provided to me in these formative years is nothing short of miraculous (the Fowler family and the Barton family, in particular). I couldn't have written a book without all the teachers along the way who helped me hone my writing skills, brought a love of words, and taught me to find passion in my content (Sharon Holderfield and Alex McAllister, I am looking at you.) Thank you to all of the friends, the boyfriends, the random people I talked to in coffee shops or bars in my 20s—all those who sparked an idea or a word pattern—the list is too long, but you know who you are.

I am grateful to Katie S. Kramer for her exceptional editing and friendship. Renée Kennedy brought excellent design work and deeper wisdom, too. I was fortunate to have a skillful copyeditor in Anali North Martin, and Jack Nestor at Technica Editorial provided support and useful information. I offer a truly sincere *thank you* to Kent Ford for the beautifully written book summary, incredible support on the writing journey, and many final revisions. Thank you for believing in me.

Elsie, my first born, you always surprise me. You bring ideas and questions into my life—words that are so very astute for a ten-year-old. The surprise is calculated, though— long and slow, even. You are thoughtful and you experience the world in a sensitive fashion like I do. Thank you for the ways you continually surprise me, with words and with music and with art. Your fire ignites my own. I am so grateful for you, and I am so proud of the person you are.

Acknowledgments

Beatrice, my little one-one: you feel so deeply. You are fast-moving and strong, and you are a deep well. Thank you for keeping me laughing, and for your raw emotions that rarely surface at this point but are so real when they do. You help me tap into that well, and I hope I will be able to do the same for you. I am so, so grateful you were born and for the amazing journey that your birth initiated. I am very proud of you, too.

Elsie and Bea, I love you far beyond all that is seen.

www.ingramcontent.com/pod-product-compliance
Lightning Source LLC
Chambersburg PA
CBHW021236130626
46554CB00004B/1521